GUIDE FOR CELEBRATING®
WORSHIP OF THE EUCHARIST OUTSIDE MASS

PREPARING PARISH WORSHIP™

JOHN THOMAS LANE, SSS

LTP

LITURGY
TRAINING
PUBLICATIONS

Nihil Obstat
Very Reverend Daniel A. Smilanic, JCD
Vicar for Canonical Services
Archdiocese of Chicago
March 25, 2015

Imprimatur
Very Reverend Ronald A. Hicks
Vicar General
Archdiocese of Chicago
March 25, 2015

LTP and the author are grateful for the additional material provided by Arthur David Canales (exposition and youth on page 81). Corinna Laughlin (Eucharistic processions on page 47 and liturgy and devotions on page 63), Jill Maria Murdy (opportunities for exposition on page 76 and Perpetual Adoration on page 45), Dennis Smolarski, SJ (number of tabernacles on page 69), Sr. Mary Esther Nickel, RSM (Eucharistic theology on pages 1–3), Mary Pat Storms (liturgical environment on page 26), and Viviane Williams (Eucharistic theology on pages 1–3) © LTP. A special thank you to Christopher J. Ferraro and the Diocese of Rockville Centre for sharing information about their diocesan Eucharistic Congress held in 2006.

PREPARING PARISH WORSHIP™: GUIDE FOR CELEBRATING® WORSHIP OF THE EUCHARIST OUTSIDE MASS © 2015 Archdiocese of Chicago: Liturgy Training Publications, 3949 South Racine Avenue, Chicago IL 60609, 1-800-933-1800; fax 1-800-933-7094; e-mail orders@ltp.org. All rights reserved. See our website at www.LTP.org.

This book was edited by Danielle A. Noe, MDiv. Christopher Magnus was the production editor, Anna Manhart was the designer, and Luis Leal was the production artist.

Cover photo courtesy St. Raphael Catholic Church, Naperville, Illinois; Art on page vii, by Martin Erspamer, OSB; Photo on page 56 by Yvette Dostatni; Photos on pages 3 and 11 are courtesy St. Mary of the Lake/Mundelein Seminary; Other photos © John Zich.

Printed in the United States of America.

20   19   18   17   16   2   3   4   5   6

Library of Congress Control Number: 2015940480

ISBN 978-1-61671-243-3

EGCEOM

CONTENTS

PREFACE

The sea was no longer calm. "This seemed like a good idea a few minutes ago," Peter thought to himself as the waves rolled under the boat, pitching them farther from the shore.[1]

"Are you sure this is a good idea?" asked Thomas.

"Definitely," said Peter, perhaps a little too quickly. "The Master plainly said, 'Go on ahead to the other side while I dismiss the crowds.'"[2]

Dismissing the crowds was no small task. The men alone had numbered five thousand, and women and children had accompanied them. Besides, incredibly, Jesus had just somehow fed all of them from five loaves and two fish.[3] In one stroke he had satisfied their hunger and whetted their appetite. The whole crowd wanted more, much more from him.

But Jesus intended to dismiss them. He wanted to be alone. "It's impossible," said Jude. "He'll never be left alone ever again."

"Well, at least he wants us," thundered James and John.

Indeed, Jesus, hungry for moments of solitude, had practically pushed the disciples into this boat with instructions to meet him on the other side.[4] The wind was already kicking up, and they were a little reluctant to set sail. But he had always been right in the past.

"What could possibly go wrong?" asked Judas. And they all got into the boat.

Now, though, it was clear that they were going nowhere. Darkness had fallen upon the sea. Gales had ripped the sail. Water had breached the side. Philip was scooping pools of water out as fast as they settled within. The disciples were afloat, but aimless.

---

1 The following is a story based on Matthew 14:13–33.
2 See Matthew 14:22.
3 See Matthew 14:13–21.
4 See Matthew 14:22.

"Where exactly are we headed?" pressed Thomas. Peter thought to himself, "I have no idea." But he said aloud, "Where Jesus wants us to be," which was not a lie.

Minutes stretched into hours. No one slept. Light finally crept across the far horizon. "I can see a little better," proclaimed Nathaniel.

But Simon the Zealot, a total stranger to fear, was staring open-mouthed into the damp thick air. "It's a ghost," he stammered.[5] "A ghost is walking on the water." The stress of the long night finally overtook them all. The other disciples started crying out in fear.

"Take courage," a voice boomed across the abyss, louder than the sea, stronger than the wind, brighter than the light, more comforting than a friend. "It is I."[6]

"How could this be?" Peter wondered. "Am I that close to the shore? How else can the Master be walking and speaking so near?"

"Do not be afraid." The words wrapped them like a blanket.

"I've heard that message before," said Matthew. "It really is the Master. He is walking on the sea."

"It can't be the Master," thought Peter. "Nobody can walk on water." Concealing his reservations no longer, he shouted toward the figure on the sea. "Lord, if it is you, command me to come to you on the water."[7] Matthew sharply turned his head. "Are you out of your mind?"

"Come,"[8] roared the voice.

No other word carried such power. They had all heard that word before. It had summoned them into service. It had beckoned them into suffering. It had promised them hope. After hearing it once, they had all responded without hesitation.

So Peter grabbed the side of the boat and planted one foot upon the water. Then the other. He started walking and came toward Jesus.[9]

Then the wind surged. The waves slapped at Peter's thighs. He became frightened and started to sink. Not just his body, but his spirit, his hopes, his self-confidence, his leadership, and his faith all began to sink beneath the

---

5 See Matthew 14:26.

6 Matthew 14:27.

7 Matthew 14:28.

8 Matthew 14:29.

9 Matthew 14:29.

waves. It was Jesus who usually commanded him, but now, drowning in desperation, Peter commanded Jesus. "Lord, save me!"[10] he screamed.

Jesus simply reached out a hand and caught him. Jesus shook his head twice and turned up the left side of his mouth. "You of little faith, why did you doubt?"[11]

To their relief, the other disciples realized he had asked this question to Peter alone, not to the group. Jesus was not questioning their faith—just Peter's. Jesus climbed into the boat and hauled his shaken friend on board. The wind ceased.[12] So did the doubts that the others had harbored, though they hoped the Master had not noticed.

The disciples looked at him, rays of light pouring into the sea behind them. Jesus' face shined like the sun. Falling back a half step, James raised a hand to shield his eyes. Nathaniel felt privileged just to be in the Master's presence.

Then they all did what you have to do when you are in the blessed presence of Jesus Christ.

They worshipped him.

They said in the calm, "Truly, you are the Son of God."[13]

Christians yearn for time at church the way the disciples craved time with Jesus. Doubts and fears do not keep us from Christ. They make us seek him all the more. Catholics derive special comfort from the Real Presence of Christ in the Blessed Sacrament. He comes to us under the form of bread and wine as miraculously as he walked upon the water. When we enter a church and behold the sacramental presence of our Lord and Master, we imitate the example of those who saw him on the sea. We worship. And believe.

—Paul Turner

---

10 See Matthew 14:30.
11 See Matthew 14:31.
12 See Matthew 14:32.
13 Matthew 14:33.

WELCOME

"Do this in memory of me."

—Luke 22:19

On the night before Jesus died, he had supper with his disciples, at which time he gave them, and us, the everlasting memorial of his Body and Blood. Since that night, Christians have remembered and celebrated Christ's risen presence throughout their lives, through participation in the Mass. As St. Paul reminds us in his First Letter to the Corinthians, every time we eat and drink of the Lord's Body, we remember.[1] Christ's giving of himself in simple bread and wine and our reception of this gift allows us to share in the mystery of salvation. Contemplating this mystery is important to our lives of faith.

Throughout the ages, Roman Catholics have pondered the mystery of and shown devotion to the Eucharist in a number of ways. Our weekly, if not daily, opportunity to feast with our Lord at Mass helps us to grow in faith and be strenghtened to give witness to God in the world. Continuing to pray after Mass in the presence of the Blessed Sacrament leads us to a deeper understanding of the Eucharist and its meaning in our lives.

Many resources have been published to aid our prayer in the presence of the Blessed Sacrament. However, aside from the ritual books, few pastoral resources are available regarding the theology and history of Eucharistic worship outside of Mass and how "to do" these rites appropriately. This resource is a practical tool written within a theological framework about worship of the Eucharist outside of Mass. It is intended for trained and volunteer pastoral staff members who prepare the liturgical and devotional life of the parishes, religious communities, campus ministries, schools, and other Catholic communities. It can be used to effectively prepare the Rite of Exposition and Benediction, Eucharistic processions, and other Eucharistic

---

1 See 1 Corinthians 11:23–27.

liturgies and devotions that are outside of Mass. This resource will be a great asset to your ministry in renewing this prayer experience for your community.

About the Author

John Thomas Lane, sss, is a religious of the Congregation of the Blessed Sacrament. After studying to be a music teacher and receiving degrees in music and education from the University of Akron, he joined religious life and professed vows of poverty, chastity, and obedience in 1988. He received a Master of Divinity with a specialization in Word and Worship from Catholic Theological Union and was ordained a presbyter in 1992. He pursued further study in liturgy, receiving a Master of Arts in Liturgical Studies at the University of Notre Dame, Indiana, in 1998. He has served the Church as a music minister, youth minister, director of an office of worship (Diocese of Salt Lake City, Utah), pastor, vocation minister, and liturgical consultant. He has published articles with *Emmanuel Magazine*, *AIM*, *Today's Liturgy*, and *Modern Liturgy* and has been a contributing author to *Sourcebook for Sundays, Seasons, and Weekdays* (LTP). Fr. Lane is a speaker at national and parish workshops and serves as a liturgical consultant. He currently pastors his home parish, St. Paschal Baylon, in Highland Heights, Ohio.

The Theology and History
of Eucharistic Worship
Outside of Mass

"Remain here and keep watch with me."

—Matthew 26:38

We use the word *Eucharist* to describe our most important Catholic liturgy—the Mass. The word is also used to refer to the Body and Blood of Christ in Holy Communion. The word *Eucharist* comes from the Greek word *eucharistein*, which means "thanksgiving" or "to give thanks" (to this day, if you want to say "thank you" in Greek you say *efharistó*!). The Mass is a great prayer of thanksgiving that the Church offers to God. We give thanks to God for all the blessings of our lives, but especially for the gift of Christ.

When we come together to celebrate the Mass, Christ is present to us in many ways—in the proclamation of the Word, in the people assembled, in the presider, and most especially, in the Eucharist.[1] The Mass is our primary act of worship as Catholics for it is the "source and summit of the christian life."[2] When we participate in Mass and receive Holy Communion, we come closer and closer to Christ and to one another. The Church's greatest liturgy, the Mass, gathers us around the table of the Lord to give thanks to God and to receive God's gift of the Body and Blood of Christ. The sacrament we receive is meant to transform us more and more into the very Body of Christ. For this reason, the Mass ends with words of mission: "*Ite, missa est*" or "Go, you are sent." We are sent, as Christ's disciples, to do the work of the Gospel in the world. We are sent as Christ's very Body, his hands and feet, to bring Christ's healing, compassion, and love to those in need—the sick, the imprisoned, the poor, and the marginalized. For those who celebrate the Eucharist, such service is not an option. In celebrating the mystery of Christ's love, the

---

1 See *Constitution on the Sacred Liturgy* (CSL), 7.
2 *Lumen gentium* (LG), 11; see also CSL, 10.

Church receives the command, and the grace, to transform our culture into a civilization of love.

Even though the Mass is our primary prayer as Catholic Christians, our prayer is not limited to Mass. Christ taught the disciples that they must pray always without becoming tired.[3] St. Paul instructed the Thessalonians to "pray without ceasing."[4] Catholics usually reserve (save) some Eucharist from each Mass. We do this because the Eucharist is as necessary for the Catholic spiritual life as ordinary food is for the body. And, we believe that Christ is present in the Eucharist as long as the consecrated bread and wine exist. From the beginning, the Church sent the Blessed Sacrament, bread or hosts consecrated at Mass, to those unable to come to Mass. This practice of sharing Communion continues today. Day after day, week after week, ministers of care bring Holy Communion to the homebound, the imprisoned, the sick, and the dying.

The Blessed Sacrament is reserved in a tabernacle. The tabernacle cannot be moved and it is always locked. It may be located in the sanctuary (somewhere near the altar) of the church or in a chapel in the church. A lamp is placed near the tabernacle and burns day and night as a reminder that Christ is present in the reserved Eucharist. The primary function of the tabernacle is practical—to protect the reserved Eucharist. But it is also a place that can help nourish people's prayer and devotion.

Over the centuries, many different forms of Eucharistic worship outside of Mass have developed. These rituals and devotions express the love the faithful have for Christ in the Blessed Sacrament and include times of adoration, Holy Hours, exposition and benediction of the Blessed Sacrament, Eucharistic processions (on Holy Thursday and the Solemnity of the Most Holy Body and Blood of Christ [*Corpus Christi*]), Eucharistic congresses, and other forms of devotional or personal prayer. The Church encourages that we express our faith in the

---

The tabernacle was first intended for the reservation of the Eucharist in a worthy place so that it could be brought to the sick and those absent, outside of Mass. As faith in the real presence of Christ in his Eucharist deepened, the Church became conscious of the meaning of silent adoration of the Lord present under the Eucharistic species.

—*Catechism of the Catholic Church*, 1379

---

3 See Luke 18:1.
4 1 Thessalonians 5:17.

Eucharist outside of Mass. This type of prayer can draw us closer to Christ and inspire us to pray for the peace and justice and the salvation of the world. The following traces the history of how these practices emerged over the Christian centuries.

Mass is celebrated at Soldier Field, Chicago, at the 28th International Eucharistic Congress in 1926.

The Early Church

The New Testament Gospel accounts and letters of St. Paul agree that the Last Supper, or the Supper of the Lord, occurred during a Passover ritual. The Passover meal included flat barley cakes, the staple food of the time, which later became the bread for Eucharistic meals.

As documented in the letters of St. Paul, especially to the Corinthians, the disciples of Christ gathered for a potluck meal, called an "agape" or love meal. The Lord's Supper followed the potluck meal. This included repeating the words of Jesus Christ on the night before he died and the sharing of the bread and the cup. The bread was kept in baskets and deacons were sent to bring this bread to those who were not present for the Eucharistic gatherings. People made the Eucharistic bread, and it represented the homemade style of their lives lived as a Eucharistic people. Because of the threat of persecution, Christians would gather in a house church (*Dura-Europas*), a borrowed space that was adaptable for the crowds.

For the early Christians, this memorial meal was a sharing in the Death and Resurrection of Christ. It was a response to the Lord's command to take and eat, but it was also a great thanksgiving and recognition

> Then he took the bread, said the blessing, broke it, and gave it to them, saying, "This is my body, which will be given for you; do this in memory of me."
>
> —Luke 22:19

of the blessings that their loving and forgiving God had bestowed upon them.

The early Church's prayer echoed the Jewish prayer rituals, keeping holy the third, sixth, and ninth hours (and others) with a short moment for prayer. It was important for the early disciples to keep the rhythm of the day and to repeat what a good Jew, like Jesus and his Apostles, would follow.

As Christians became settled in their own rhythm of keeping time holy, they also moved the focus of gathering to pray from the Sabbath (present-day Saturday) to the Lord's Day (Day of the Resurrection, Sunday). From the start, the people of God gathered and grew in their understanding of themselves as the Body of Christ, praying, worshipping, and being together with the head of the Body—Christ the Lord.

There are records of early Christian prayer texts regarding the way the Eucharist was celebrated in peoples' homes, with the leader of the home having his own style of praying while leading the celebration. The Eucharist was a way of life. It included going into the community to live the Gospel, and, at times, even die for Gospel values.

In 180 AD, St. Peter's relics were found on Vatican Hill and these relics were kept sacred. Those who died for Christ were lifted up as early heroes. A *refrigerium*, or, a special tomb, was placed on the burial place of St. Peter. Other catacombs and sacred sites of the martyrs were kept private for the Christian community to pray and share a meal. This practice led to the construction of buildings that were used for worship. To highlight the importance of the burial sites, frescoes depicting their deaths were painted on the ceilings and walls. In these houses, or catacombs, a single cupboard, closet, or chest was used to reserve the Eucharist and the Scriptures for the weekly gathering. Members of the community, especially deacons, would bring Communion to those who were unable to come to the Lord's Day services. The bread would be placed in an *arcae*, the precursor to the pyx, and worn around the neck in order to share the Eucharistic meal with the sick. By the third century, other liturgical items were made from precious metals and other materials. Permanent spaces, purchased spaces, and imperial buildings were becoming used as a place for worship.

In 313 AD, Emperor Constantine legalized Christianity in the Roman Empire. Christians no longer feared to publically worship, and the celebration of the Eucharist became the most common form of public worship attended on Sunday and other feast days. Worship moved from home settings to more permanent, public, or formal "basilica" style buildings. As buildings and sacred shrines were built at the important places of Christianity (especially those important in the lives of Christ and the apostles), the architecture of the building became fixed. In these new designs, the altar is farther away and more remote, usually designed to be at one end of the basilica hall.

The Medieval Period

As the Western Church communities grew and larger crowds gathered for worship, the Eucharistic bread was made in large quantities and divided into smaller pieces, thus, looking less like a loaf of bread. New containers, called patens, were made to hold the bread. Some patens were so large they had to be held by two special ministers, or acolytes. A smaller container, the pyx, was used to hold Communion for the sick. Tabernacles were constructed and placed within churches. The tabernacles were often shaped in the form of a dove and hung in a sacristy or preparation room.

During the eighth to eleventh centuries, there was great development in the order or format of the Eucharistic celebration and its corresponding theology. Much of this development can be traced to monastic communities of religious men who were celebrating the Eucharist daily, beyond the Lord's Day (Sunday). These communities were able to include private intentions for the dead, causing a major shift in the understanding and purpose of gathering as a community of faith. What had been primarily a meal remembering Christ's Passion, Death, and Resurrection, was now a prayer primarily for remembering the dead.

In 831 AD, a theological debate occured regarding Christ's Real Presence in the Eucharist. This debate would significantly influence the Church's understanding of the Eucharist. Paschasius Radbertus, Abbot of the monastery of Corbie, France, wrote that Christians eat the *very bodily flesh* of Christ and drink his *very bodily blood*. His literal understanding was heavily influenced by the accounts of Eucharistic miracles, such as bleeding hosts. Ratramnus, a monk of the same abbey, disagreed with Radbertus. Instead, Ratramnus claimed that Christ's presence was real, but not in a physical way. Christ's presence in the Eucharist was his resurrected, glorified body. It is this latter theological view that would be adoped by the Church.[5]

During a ninth century council, the bishops of Rouen, France, directed that the Eucharist could not be placed in the hand of any layperson. They must receive Communion on the tongue. The faithful also began to feel

---

5 See Nathan Mitchell, *Cult and Controversy: The Worship of the Eucharist Outside Mass.* Collegeville, MN: Liturgical Press, 1982; page 81.

unworthy and disconnected from Christ, and many no longer regularly received Communion.

As the reception of Communion and participation in the Mass diminished, devotion to the saints grew, as did other practices related to the saints, such as the Rosary. Popular devotions grew across Europe as pilgrimages were made to visit relics of holy people, which were being transferred across the Roman Empire.

Monastic communities began making unleavened Eucharistic bread. The pieces became smaller, partly because of the fewer numbers of people who were receiving Communion, but also due to the growing concern from the people that they were chewing the actual flesh and bones of Christ.

Church buildings were reconstructed with areas sectioned off with rood screens. The screens prevented the lay faithful from being close to the altar. Church architecture now reflected the hierarchical structure of the Church— the ordained in one area, and the laity in another. In many instances, the priest began to celebrate the Mass with his back to the people, since churches were not necessarily built to face to East (the place of Resurrection), as had been the previous custom.

Patens became smaller, only large enough to hold the host for the priest. In the ninth century, the term *ciborium* also began to be used for this same vessel. Baskets were no longer used because the Eucharistic food was no longer in the form of bread. Additionally, chalices and vessels became more precious than the community itself, and were blessed with special prayers before the vessels were used at Mass. Household vessels were no longer used.

The Forty Hours devotion originated in the late medieval period and is linked to Holy Thursday. For forty hours from Holy Thursday until Holy Saturday, people took turns praying in front of the altar where the sacrament was reserved. In his treatise, *On the Trinity*, St. Augustine said this timing was significant because Jesus lay in the tomb for forty hours.

It could be stated that during the medieval era, the presence of Christ in the Blessed Sacrament was amplified while the presence of Christ in the Word and assembly diminished. With the growing popularity of devotion to the relics of the martyrs and saints, the same could be said to be true for the Eucharist. The Eucharist was now becoming a relic of Christ.

The custom of visiting the reserved sacrament in various churches began in the eleventh century. In Orleans, France, Bishop Jonas (†844) had written about the importance of visiting churches where the relics were kept in order to pray. In the eleventh century, this practice soon transferred from praying with the relics of the martyrs to praying with the Body of Christ. The declining numbers of people receiving Communion and the greater sense of unworthiness contributed to the Eucharist becoming the ultimate relic.

Until the thirteenth century, relics were reserved in the principal altar of the church. Now, tabernacles housing the Blessed Sacrament were placed on the altars. The Fourth Lateran Council in 1215 instructed that churches must keep the tabernacles locked at all times. This was to prevent people from taking the Blessed Sacrament for their own personal use.

The doctrine of concomitance was established at this time. "Concomitance" means that Christ is entirely present in bread *or* wine, and that in receiving one species one receives both.

Ocular Communion, or the practice of gazing upon the host to become one with Christ, became the norm. Looking upon the consecrated host became a satisfactory way of participating in the Mass. Because people were rarely attending the entire Mass or receiving Communion, bells began to be rung at certain times during the Mass. This alerted the people in town that it was almost time to go to church to gaze upon the host. In 1206, a synod in Paris demanded that the priest elevate the Eucharist so that the people could see the host. The practice of "seeing and adoring" is the impetus for viewing the host at other times beyond the Mass. This led to the development of transparent vessels, or monstrances, and the ritual of exposition.

During the thirteenth century, St. Thomas Aquinas wrote extensively about the Eucharist as a sacrament and symbol. He taught that the Eucharist was a sign (*Sacramentum tantum*) of an underlying reality (*res tantum*) that effects in us God's grace (*res sacramenti*). Christ's presence was real, substantial, and sacramental. Aquinas contextualized the Eucharistic mystery with Aristotelian philosophy: "accident unchanged, substance changed."[6] Aquinas' theological explanations of the Eucharist had a lasting impact, and form the basis of what we know and understand today. Because of Aquinas' theology, the Council of Trent defined transubstantiation and encouraged devotion to the Eucharist. With transubstantiation, the accidents of the bread and wine remain, but the substance is changed into the Body, Blood, soul, and divinity of Christ. Transubstantiation became the penultimate expression of Roman Catholic theology on the Eucharist.

---

6 From the Council of Trent, decree concerning the Most Holy Sacrament of the Eucharist, canon II, citing St. Thomas Aquinas.

During this era, Eucharistic piety, Eucharistic superstitions, and the desire for miracles was intensified. The faithful were convinced that the Eucharist had magical properties and they preferred miraculous explanations about the power of the host ("You won't go blind if you see the host.") They also understood the rubrics and the gestures of the Mass to magically change the bread into Christ. There was also tremendous preoccupation with death, largely due to the overwhelming health problems of the time, especially the great plagues. The hope to receive Holy Communion on one's deathbed (the so-called "Last Rites") was increasing in practice and becoming a necessity. Spirituality became focused on the internal life (*devotio moderna*), with the Eucharist as a source or focus of this prayer and need.

Processing through the community with the Blessed Sacrament was linked to the establishment of the Feast of *Corpus Christi*, or the Feast of the Body of Christ, in thirteenth-century Liège, Belgium.

In 1208, a young religious sister named Juliana began to see visions and have dreams of the Lord:

> "She saw a lunar disk surrounded by rays of dazzling white light; on one side of the disk, however, there was a dark spot that spoiled the beauty of the whole. The Lord explained to her that the dark spot meant that the Church still lacked a solemn feast in honor of the Blessed Sacrament."[7]

Juliana shared these visions with her confessor. She felt that the Lord was giving her an understanding of an annual feast to honor the sacrament of the altar, and that on this day each year the faithful should receive both the Body and Blood of Christ. Although Sr. Juliana's request for the feast provoked mixed reactions on the part of the theologians and bishops, it was well received by Bishop Robert of Liège, who celebrated the feast for the first time in 1246. Pope Urban IV (1261–1264), advanced the cause for this feast as a universal celebration.

Juliana did not foresee how the idea of the celebration of a feast for the Eucharist would grow into such pageantry, including a procession with the Eucharist through the streets of the towns. The first Eucharistic procession occured in Cologne, France between 1274 and 1279. This practice spread from village to village, in part because of the masterful, colorful pageantry with hymns, benedictions, and outdoor altars (called stations). By the

---

7 Adrian Nocent. *The Liturgical Year: Volume Three: The Paschal Triduum, The Easter Season.* Collegeville, MN: Liturgical Press, 1977; page 291.

fourteenth century, the Eucharistic procession had become popular in many areas. In 1316, Pope John XXII decreed that the procession was to be an obligatory part of the *Corpus Christi* celebration. Today, the Solemnity of the Most Holy Body and Blood[8] still includes the annual procession with the Blessed Sacrament (*Corpus Christi*).

The monstrance, in which the host had been placed, was carried under a festive canopy, preceded by all the clergy and followed by the civil authorities. An especially large host was used so that people could gaze upon the sacrament.

Many architects concede that as monstrances developed and there became greater desire to gaze upon the Blessed Sacrament, churches were built to look like the floor plan of a monstrance—cruciform in shape with domes above the center. The altar was raised higher to compensate for the longer nave. An elaborate reredos and tabernacle were constructed to emphasize the sacred host, and priests were encouraged to "show off the host" with higher elevations with the ringing of bells at special moments during the Canon (Eucharistic Prayer). The laity participated at Mass with their own devotions and prayers from their hearts.

Modernity

During the seventeenth century, Eucharistic piety continued to grow and develop. The assembly could not receive Communion for many reasons: priests were not offering daily Mass and celebrated more "private Masses" without an assembly; the faithful continued to feel unworthy and were not physically receiving Communion; priests did not feel the faithful were worthy to receive. The Latin language also contributed to this feeling of unworthiness, since the faithful could not understand what was taking place. Churches were also built so that the primary focus was upon the tabernacle rather than the altar. The Mass became the exclusive prayer of the hierarchy; exposition became the prayer of the people.

During the nineteenth century, the Vatican Congregation of Rites (now called the Congregation for Divine Worship and Discipline of the Sacraments) ruled that the tabernacle was to be attached to the main altar unless a chapel

---

8 After the Feast of *Corpus Christi* was added to the Church calendar, the Feast of the Most Precious Blood was added to the calendar in the late 1800s. The liturgical calendar reform of 1969 combined these two feasts to become the Solemnity of the Most Holy Body and Blood of Christ, an observance that now embraces the full species of the sacramental elements.

for Eucharistic reservation was available. In this case, the tabernacle was to be fixed to the main altar in the reservation chapel (such as in great basilicas). This was also at the same time that the practice of reserving the Eucharist in the sacristy was forbidden. Monstrances became more important than the altar. The altar became the place for the monstrance, rather than the place for the sacrifice of the Mass. The monstrances were so large that they needed to be placed on wheels so they could be easily transported into church. The sheer size and magnificence of the monstrances led people to believe that this was the primary form of worship.

The Forty Hours devotion grew in popularity and importance as did other opportunities for exposition throughout the year. Forty Hours and exposition often included dramatic or apologetic preaching. This style of preaching often emphasized the sharp contrasts between Catholic and Protestant theologies and became an opportunity to cause the faithful to become fearful about the pains of hell and how to achieve salvation. Forty Hours, exposition, and dramatic preaching became times of great conversion for parishes.

In the late nineteenth century, the bishops of the United States began to restore the focus on the Mass and its importance in the life of the Church. At the Second Plenary Council of Baltimore, Maryland, in 1866, the United States bishops supported heightened devotion to the Blessed Sacrament and encouraged the faithful to visit churches to pray in the presence of the Eucharist. However, the Council advised that the Eucharist was not *solely an object of adoration*, but was *spiritual food to be eaten and consumed*. The popular Forty Hours devotion now became an opportunity for preaching about participating at Mass and the importance of receiving Communion. Many priests, especially the "apostle of the Eucharist," St. Peter Julian Eymard (1811–1868)[9] began to promote a more loving approach to the Eucharist, emphasizing the importance of receiving Communion in order to be holy and loving disciples of Christ.

St. Peter Julian Eymard advocated for a universal gathering of people from around the world to attend a retreat focused on various themes of the Eucharist. These gatherings would be called Eucharistic congresses. The First International Eucharistic Congress did not take place until after Eymard's

9 Eymard founded the Congregation of the Blessed Sacrament (religious men), the Servants of the Blessed Sacrament (religious women) and the Aggregation of the Blessed Sacrament (a community of lay people) in France in the middle of the nineteenth century.

death. It was carried on by a student of Eymard, Marie Marthe Emilia Tamisier (1834–1910), a novice of the Servants of the Blessed Sacrament. It was held at the University of Lille, France, in 1881. Tamisier received approval for this gathering from Pope Leo XIII. Prior to this international meeting, local congresses had been held in France at Paray-le-Monial (1873), Avignon (1874), Faverney (around 1876), and Douai (1878). Marie Tamisier organized many pilgrimages to Eucharistic congresses and encouraged that these be regular events around the world.

Native Alaskans walk in a procession with the Eucharist at the 28th International Eucharistic Congress held in Chicago in 1926.

These congresses were seminars, or study days, with speakers on different aspects of the Eucharist—theology, pastoral ministry, and the social dimension. The congresses included exposition of the Blessed Sacrament.

As the congresses developed, the social dynamics of the Eucharist and the theology of the Church evolved, and the papers that the speakers presented became available for the universal Church to access. The 28th International Eucharistic Congress was held in Chicago in 1926. This congress, the first to be held in the United States, was hosted by George Cardinal Mundelein. It drew more than 500,000 people for the Mass at Soldier Field.[10] Hosting events of this magnitude fostered particular movements such as liturgy and justice, international peace, and so on. In this post-Conciliar Church, Eucharistic congresses continue to be encouraged. They are held on the local and international level. The most recent international congress took place in Dublin, Ireland, in 2012. The theme of the 50th International Eucharistic Congress was "The Eucharist: Communion with Christ and with one another."

---

10 Visit this website for video footage of the congress in Chicago: https://vimeo.com/3258385.

The Twentieth Century and the Reforms of the Second Vatican Council

The reform of the liturgy and our understanding of the Eucharist began to take shape in earnest during the twentieth century. Scholars began exploring ancient liturgical practices and sought to restore the rites to their original purity and simplicity. They were concerned especially about encouraging the faithful to participate in the Mass—the Eucharist—as the primary source of faith.

> The eucharistic mystery is truly the center of the liturgy and indeed of the whole Christian life.
>
> —*Eucharisticum mysterium*, 1

Several influential documents written during this time greatly impacted contemporary practice and reform. In 1910, Pope Pius X (1903–1914) promulgated *Quam singulari*. In this document, the pope advocated for the frequent reception of Communion and he lowered the age of first Communion to the "age of reason," which is around the age of seven. Pope Pius X also called for active participation in the rites of the Church, especially the Mass, which is the true source of the Christian spirit.

Pope Pius XII (1939–1958) wrote two significant documents that helped articulate the role of worship in the life and mission of the church, *Mystici Corporis Christi* (1943) and *Mediator Dei* (1947). Pius XII acknowledged the movements that were occurring in the study of the Church, especially in liturgical research, and endorsed reforms. The liturgy, the Eucharist, and popular devotions would come to the forefront of the Church's life with the Second Vatican Council, called by Pope John XXIII. Between 1962 and 1965, bishops from all over the world met at various sessions to bring the Church into the modern world. With its very first document, the *Constitution on the Sacred Liturgy,* the Council sought to renew the liturgical life of the Church so that all the faithful would be brought to "full, conscious, and active participation"[11] in the various rites. All the Church's rites were to be evaluated, simplified, and restored to their original intent and form. This included popular devotions, which were to be revised so that they would "be in harmony with the liturgy and the liturgical seasons."[12]

---

11 CSL, 14.
12 CSL, 13.

After the Second Vatican Council, the task of revising the rites of the Church began. Bishops from English-speaking countries created an international group of translators and experts called the International Commission on English in the Liturgy (ICEL). Several documents were issued concerning the "right implementation of the *Constitution on the Sacred Liturgy*." The fifth such document was *Eucharisticum mysterium*, issued in 1967. This document was written to give instructions about the Eucharist and establish norms for worship. The document reminds the Church of the central importance of the Eucharistic mystery in the life of the faithful and encourages them to frequently receive both species at Mass. The document also provides a rationale for worship of the Eucharist outside of Mass, and gives regulations for its practice so that Eucharistic piety would not distract the faithful from the liturgy.

Although *Eucharisticum mysterium* provides a rich theology of the Eucharist, and established certain norms and regulations, it did not provide a particular ritual or order of service. The order of service is provided in the 1973 ritual book, *Holy Communion and Worship of the Eucharist Outside Mass,* and the 1994 ritual book from the United States, the *Order for the Solemn Exposition of the Holy Eucharist.* Both ritual books draw heavily on the theology presented in *Eucharisticum mysterium.* An overview of the rituals presented in these two books will be explored in the next chapter.

Eucharistic devotions were not part of the life of the Church during the first millennium. Toward the end of the eleventh century, Eucharistic piety and devotion began to develop in the Western Church; eventually shifting the focus from the liturgy to personal devotions. The liturgical renewal and study that occured during the twentieth century and the reforms of the Second Vatican Council have reshaped and restored our understanding of the Eucharist and how we participate in its mysteries fully, actively, and consciously.[13]

> The Church earnestly desires that all the faithful be led to that full, conscious, and active participation in liturgical celebrations called for by the very nature of the liturgy. Such participation by the Christian people as "a chosen race, a royal priesthood, a holy nation, God's own people" (1 Pt 2:9; see 2:4–5) is their right and duty by reason of their baptism.
>
> In the reform and promotion of the liturgy, this full and active participation by all the people is the aim to be considered before all else.
>
> —*Constitution on the Sacred Liturgy,* 14

---

13 See CSL, 14.

It is this participation in the Eucharistic mysteries from which our devotional life flows.

Author's Note

I would like to acknowledge the various publications that I have read and consulted, and the courses and workshops that I have attended in order to present on this topic and write this chapter in *Guide for Celebrating® Eucharistic Worship Outside Mass.* These resources and educational opportunities have served as the basis for this work and an ongoing outline of liturgical history and diary that I created and have used for this *Guide,* and also as the source of many workshops and classes that I have taught from 1994 to the present. Special thanks to Edward Foley, Capuchin, for his Liturgical History course at the University of Notre Dame (summer, 1994). Also at Notre Dame, special thanks to Michael Driscoll, for the course on Eucharist (summer, 1996). Nathan Mitchell presented a workshop/retreat on "Eucharist: From Adoration to Evangelization" to our Congregation of the Blessed Sacrament, USA Province (winter, 2006), and Gil Ostdiek, OFM, (winter, 2007) on a similar retreat theme. I especially welcomed many conversations with Fr. Ostdiek regarding worship of the Eucharist outside of Mass at various Q&A sessions, walks, and table fellowship. In addition to these courses, workshops, and retreats, the following books were used to compile this chapter:

Foley, Edward. *From Age to Age: How Christians Have Celebrated the Eucharist.* Chicago, IL: Liturgy Training Publications, 1991.

_____, *From Age to Age: How Christians Have Celebrated the Eucharist, Revised and Expanded Edition.* Collegeville, MN: The Liturgical Press, 2008.

LaVerdiere, Eugene. *The Eucharist in the New Testament and Early Church.* Collegeville, MN: The Liturgical Press, 1996.

Mitchell, Nathan. *Cult and Controversy: The Worship of the Eucharist Outside Mass.* Collegeville, MN: The Liturgical Press, 1982.

_____. *Real Presence: The Work of Eucharist.* Chicago, IL: Liturgy Training Publications, 1998.

Rubin, Miri. *Corpus Christi: The Eucharist in Late Medieval Culture.* Cambridge, England: Cambridge University Press, 1992.

Seasoltz, R. Kevin. *Living Bread, Saving Cup: Readings on the Eucharist.* Collegeville, MN: The Liturgical Press, 1982.

I am very grateful to these scholars for their academic study and research that were the foundation for this work and my ongoing research and writing.

—John Thomas Lane, sss

Preparing Opportunities
for Prayer in the Presence
of the Blessed Sacrament

"Lord our God,
may we always give due honor
to the sacramental presence of the Lamb
who was slain for us.
May our faith be rewarded
by the vision of his glory,
who lives and reigns for ever and ever."

— *Order for the Solemn Exposition of the Blessed Sacrament*, 129, C

As we have seen, the reservation of the Blessed Sacrament and related devotions has been a part of Catholic tradition for centuries. Christ is truly present in the Eucharistic elements of bread and wine, and so the Church has encouraged particular worship and devotion to the Eucharist. In addition to the celebration of Mass, Eucharistic devotions are important for the life of the parish for they "[invite] us to the spiritual union with him that culminates in sacramental communion."[1] This means that prayer in the presence of the Blessed Sacrament (public and private) invites us into deeper participation in the Eucharistic mysteries at Mass for "the celebration of the eucharist is the center of the entire Christian life."[2]

This chapter will help you prepare gatherings of prayer in the presence of the Blessed Sacrament outside of Mass, both liturgically and personally. Eucharistic worship outside of Mass is a special way to have your community extend their prayer time with the Eucharist.

Before reviewing the specific rituals and other opportunities for prayer, it is helpful to understand the terminology associated with prayer in the presence of the Blessed Sacrament. There is a difference between personal devotion to the Eucharist and the public rituals that occur outside of Mass.

---

1 *Holy Communion and Worship of the Eucharist Outside Mass* (HCW), 82.
2 HCW, 1; see also LG, 11 and CSL, 10.

Frequently, the term "Eucharistic adoration" is used to refer to all forms of Eucharistic worship outside of Mass. But there is a difference between personal piety and the liturgical rites. The following is helpful for understanding the nuances in terminology:

1. **Adoration**: "Adoration" is a general term used to describe prayer in the presence of the Blessed Sacrament. It is an act of devotion. The Sacrament may be exposed for the purpose of adoration or the faithful may gather in prayer in the presence of the Sacrament reserved in the tabernacle.

2. **Perpetual Adoration**: Perpetual adoration is devotional prayer that is repeatedly done with Church members attending to specific hours in the presence of the reserved Blessed Sacrament in front of or near the tabernacle. For centuries, Church members were encouraged to "make a visit" for some period of time so that Christ could be praised and all could prepare for his return. Because the Sacrament is not exposed, parishes are not required to receive permission from the bishop when offering perpetual adoration.

3. **Exposition and Benediction**: The Rite of Exposition and Benediction is a liturgical rite of the Catholic Church during which a larger host is consecrated at Mass and later placed in a ciborium or monstrance for communal prayer. It does involve adoration— following the act of exposition, the gathered faithful continue to pray communally in the presence of the exposed Sacrament with Scripture readings, singing, prayer, and silence. Benediction concludes the service with the blessing of the gathered faithful with the host exposed in the monstrance. The rite itself does not require permission from the bishop. Permission is only required if the Sacrament is continuously exposed (see number 4 below).

4. **Perpetual Exposition**: The Eucharist is exposed or visible in the monstrance for an extended period of time. This requires permission from the local bishop.

A distinction should be made between adoration of the reserved Blessed Sacrament and exposition of the Blessed Sacrament. Eucharistic adoration of the reserved Blessed Sacrament is a devotional act. Eucharistic exposition is a liturgical action, by which the Blessed Sacrament is displayed outside the tabernacle in a monstrance or ciborium for public veneration by the faithful. It is a public celebration that enables the faithful to perceive more clearly the relationship between the reserved Sacrament and [the Mass].

—*Sing to the Lord: Music in Divine Worship*, 242

Eucharistic worship outside of Mass is an important part of parish life.

5. **Eucharistic Processions**: A procession with the Blessed Sacrament exposed in the monstrance. It may move beyond the church and into the streets.

6. **Eucharistic Congress**: A gathering of the local or international Church to study the Eucharist, celebrate the Mass, and pray in the presence of the Blessed Sacrament.

7. **Forty Hours**: The Blessed Sacrament is exposed for forty hours, more or less.[3]

8. **Holy Hour**: One hour of prayer in the presence of the Blessed Sacrament. The Sacrament may or may not be exposed. It may be liturgical or a private devotion.

The terms above are often used interchangeably, yet it should be pointed out that "perpetual adoration" may be done continuously in a chapel where the Blessed Sacrament is reserved in the tabernacle. Most parishes actually promote "perpetual exposition" where the Blessed Sacrament is exposed in a monstrance on the altar of a chapel, while members of the parish take turns praying in the presence of the Blessed Sacrament. It is helpful to remember that specifically setting up a chapel for perpetual *exposition* of the Blessed

---

3 It could be less than forty hours because of the number of Masses and special services going on in the Church, which require you to temporarily cease exposition and return the Eucharist to the tabernacle.

Sacrament requires permission from the bishop. However, perpetual *adoration* does not require the bishop's permission.

Parish Team

Before beginning to prepare the liturgies and other devotional opportunities for members of the parish to pray in the presence of the Blessed Sacrament, a preparation team should be formed. If a parish does not have a "standing" or existing committee or commission that prepares the liturgy, the pastor and other members of the staff (primarily liturgical staff) should begin the process of discernment and gather volunteers to assist in this vital effort. Other resources and people can assist you in developing a liturgy commission or committee. However, a special "subcommittee" or new group that is interested in promoting worship of the Eucharist outside of Mass could be formed to assist in the preparation for such a ministry in the parish. Ask for a representative from parish organizations involving prayer, vocations, liturgy, pastoral council, finance, music, and youth ministry to be present to then serve as a liaison or outreach to particular groups in the parish. Members of the team should be persons of prayer and be familiar with the liturgical documents and norms of the Church. The team should review the options the Church provides for Eucharist worship outside Mass and determine what is possible for their particular parish.

Even though this core team is responsible for preparing the details surrounding Eucharistic worship outside Mass—scheduling, publicity, selecting Scripture passages and music, preparing the environment—this team is essentially establishing a "community at prayer" for the parish. This is a modern term that highlights the parish's or shrine's prayer ministry and includes those who are coming to church or the chapel to pray in the presence of the Blessed Sacrament and those who are homebound praying at their residence.[4]

---

4 The term "community at prayer" comes from the theology of St. Peter Julian Eymard, the "apostle of the Eucharis" and founder of the Aggregation of the Blessed Sacrament (lay associates), the Servants of the Blessed Sacrament (religious women), and the Congregation of the Blessed Sacrament (religious brothers, deacons, and priests).

Another important pastoral reason for stressing the phrase, "community at prayer," is for those who are unable to come to a chapel, church, or shrine and pray because they are homebound or have health reasons that keep them from coming to a church building to pray. Our prayer time, while important at the local "holy site," unites us even when we are in a home or hospital and we can remain faithful to our hour of prayer when our physical limitations keep us away.

Publicity and Catechesis

A person on the pastoral team should be designated to work with the parish bulletin and website editor(s) and the person who makes the announcements at weekend Masses, as well as informing other parish bulletin and website editors and diocesan newspapers about the parish schedule for Eucharistic worship opportunities. Ideally, when there are regional gatherings of priests (such as deanery, vicariate, or district meetings), a priest, deacon, or other leader from the parish should inform the group of the starting date and time of exposition of the Blessed Sacrament in a parish, a chapel, or regular celebrations of worship outside of Mass. Regional or group support helps the collaborative efforts for promoting this type of prayer.

The pastoral team should decide upon how they will catechize the faithful about the devotional life of the Church and its important connection to the Mass. The team should also review resources to make available for parishioners in the church vestibule for people to use during prayer, as well as providing pastoral explanations in the Sunday bulletin or post on the parish website.[5] Priests and deacons might consider ways to integrate catechesis in their homilies, especially homilies offered at exposition or at Masses preceding exposition.[6]

Reviewing the Ritual Books

The Church provides two ritual books that may be used when preparing formal, communal rituals with the Blessed Sacrament. Parish teams should be familiar with the regulations and rituals provided in *Holy Communion and Worship of the Eucharist Outside Mass* and the *Order for the Solemn Exposition of the Holy Eucharist*.[7]

Holy Communion and Worship of the Eucharist Outside Mass was promulgated (mandated for liturgical use) in 1973, and it was the first ritual

---

5 Many of the pastoral ideas provided on page 59 under "Eucharistic Congresses" may also be used or adapted to catechize the faithful regularly about the Eucharist.

6 See page 54.

7 In addition to these ritual books, it will be helpful to be familiar with *The Roman Missal* (RM), the *Lectionary for Mass* (LM), and the *Ceremonial of Bishops* (CB). This is explained in more detail below (see page 24). Parish teams should also be familiar with liturgical documents providing legislation for the liturgical and devotional life of the Church such as the *Constitution on the Sacred Liturgy* (CSL), *Redemptionis sacramentum* (RS), *General Instruction of the Roman Missal* (GIRM), *Built of Living Stones* (BLS), *Sing to the Lord: Music in Divine Worship* (STL), and the *Directory on Popular Piety and the Liturgy* (DPPL). Other, more theological documents, such as *Ecclesia de Eucharistia* (EE) and *Sacramentum caritatis* (SacCar) will also be helpful.

book following the Second Vatican Council specifically outlining the rituals for worshipping the Eucharist outside of Mass. These rituals include distributing Holy Communion outside of Mass, especially to the dying and the sick (for ordained and lay ministers)[8]; the Rite of Eucharistic Exposition and Benediction[9]; as well as Eucharistic processions[10] and Eucharistic congresses.[11] The ritual book provides a basic model for the Rite of Exposition and Benediction and suggests alternative prayers and suggested Scripture passages.

The Order for the Solemn Exposition of the Holy Eucharist was developed by the United States Conference of Catholic Bishops for the dioceses of the United States and was published by the Liturgical Press in 1993. It expands upon *Holy Communion and Worship of the Eucharist Outside Mass* (often quoting full texts of this document) and presents complete orders of services for various forms of exposition and benediction. This ritual book is primarily meant to be used "for a period lasting one or several days according to local custom or pastoral need," especially for the Forty Hours devotion,[12] and provides "periods for liturgical prayer during [day or days] the period of exposition" with "three types of services": the Liturgy of the Hours during exposition,[13] Eucharistic services of prayer and praise,[14] and the celebration of Mass during the period of exposition.[15] This includes prayer texts, expanded rubrics, Scripture texts, and hymns. The services in this ritual book can also be used and adapted for shorter periods of Exposition.

Rite of Eucharistic Exposition and Benediction

As with all forms of Eucharistic piety, the purpose of the Rite of Exposition is to invite the faithful into deeper communion with Christ and to lead the faithful to a deeper participation at Mass when receiving Christ in Communion. The tabernacle may be opened so that the ciborium (a covered vessel holding the Eucharist) is revealed. Or, a consecrated host may be placed in a special holder, called a monstrance, so it can be clearly seen by the people.

---

8 Please note that this guide book does not include information about distributing Holy Communion outside Mass.

9 See below.

10 See page 47.

11 See page 58.

12 See page 44.

13 See page 37.

14 See page 24.

15 See page 29.

This may be done by a bishop, priest, deacon, or layperson. The period for exposition may last less than an hour or may last for many hours or days. The Sacrament exposed in the monstrance is the most common form. Exposition occurs so we might feel closer to Christ and can pray more intensely. Since the reserved Sacrament comes from the celebration of the Eucharist, exposition reminds us that the Mass is our highest form of worship.

Theme

When deciding on what prayers, readings, and music to select, it might be helpful to pick a theme for the entire service. Sometimes a particular focus or theme will assist those who are gathering and awaken their challenge to grow in holiness for a particular issue or need. For instance, parish organizations (Social Concerns Committee, Knights of Columbus, St. Vincent de Paul Society, Vocation Committee, ProLife Group, Rosary and Altar Society) may have a particular need or concern that they wish to bring to prayer in the presence of the Blessed Sacrament. Rotate particular needs as part of the prayer life of the parish. Additionally, scheduling exposition on particular holidays or anniversaries will draw other aspects of our Eucharistic living into communion with our prayer.[16]

The *Catechism of the Catholic Church* describes the many themes that are part of the Eucharist and Eucharistic living: union with Christ, unity of Christians, commitment to the poor, pledge of the glory to come, and so on.[17] These themes can help guide your preparations and selections of Scripture readings, music, and prayer texts.

In . . . exposition care must be taken that everything clearly brings out the meaning of eucharistic worship in its correlation with the Mass. There must be nothing about the appointments used for exposition that could in any way obscure Christ's intention of instituting the eucharist above all to be near us to feed, to heal, and to comfort us.

—*Holy Communion and Worship of the Eucharist Outside Mass*, 82

---

16 For example, January 1 is the World Day of Prayer for Peace; September 11 is Patriot Day; November 2 is All Souls' Day; November 30 is the Feast of St. Andrew (patron saint of vocations), and so on.

17 See the *Catechism of the Catholic Church* (CCC), 1322–1419.

Readings, Music, and Prayer Texts

Both *Holy Communion and Worship of the Eucharistic Outside Mass* and *Order for the Solemn Exposition of the Holy Eucharist* are clear that Scripture, music, silence, and prayers should be included in every celebration of worship of the Eucharist outside of Mass. The ritual books provide full orders of services; however, Scripture texts other than the ones provided in the ritual books may be used. The ritual books also provide alternate Scripture suggestions[18] and the *Order for Solemn Exposition of the Holy Eucharist* even includes suggested music with four-part harmony arrangements.[19]

The *Lectionary for Mass* is another good source for finding Scripture texts. For particular saints, readings have already been chosen and included in the Lectionary for these days. The fourth volume of the Lectionary also provides readings for Masses for various needs and occasions such as for the Church, religious, and vocations; and public needs for peace, justice, and reconciliation. The Lectionary also includes Scripture texts for Masses for various public circumstances such as the beginning of the civil year, for productive land, harvests, refugees, the sick, earthquakes, and so on. Even though the readings in the Lectionary are primarily for use at Mass, you may use the same readings at Eucharistic services that are outside of Mass.

Both *Holy Communion and Worship of the Eucharist Outside Mass*[20] and the *Order for the Solemn Exposition of the Holy Eucharist*[21] include alternative antiphons, litanies, and prayers to use. *The Roman Missal* is a good source for alternative prayers to begin and end the service. This is in addition to those found in the ritual books. The Missal will be especially helpful for services on particular saints' days. You could also use texts from the Votive Masses of the Holy Eucharist and the Mass for the Solemnity of the Most Holy Body and Blood of Christ (*Corpus Christi).*

Many hymnals and music resources are organized by themes. The Eucharistic songs or hymns are usually in the "Eucharist" section which makes it easy to select songs. Other appropriate themes are "Praise" and "Thanksgiving." The themes are often printed on the top margin of each page in the hymnal. The music that is chosen should already be in the parish's repertoire and reflect Catholic Eucharistic theology and the particular theme

---

18 See chapter IV in HCW and the appendices in OSE.
19 See the appendices in OSE.
20 See HCW beginning at article 200.
21 See Appendix II in OSE.

or idea that will be selected for the prayer service. The parish music director should be consulted when selecting music.

Liturgical Ministers

A sacristan (or an altar server) will be helpful with setting up for exposition. Ask someone who regularly takes care of the "housekeeping" parts of the church sacristy to assist. This person prepares the necessary vessels (for example, the monstrance, luna, candles, thurible, boat, and so on) lights, sound system, and other items (such as heat and air conditioning).

During a service, one to three altar servers could be present to serve as crossbearers, candle bearers, book bearers, and thurifers. If exposition includes a procession, you will need servers to help carry the canopy, as well as two candle bearers. You might need addi-

tional servers depending upon how elaborate the procession will be. If the procession is elaborate, it might be best to schedule older teens or adult servers to help.[22]

Sacristans, servers, and presiders should be aware of how the monstrance works and how the latches fasten before the service begins.

Parish readers should be scheduled to serve. Be sure to give

A sacristan readies the monstrance for exposition of the Blessed Sacrament.

them the readings ahead of time so that they can prepare to proclaim God's Word. Cantors, psalmists, and other parish musicians should also be available and prepared

In selecting a presider, work with the pastor. If the pastor leads the preparation team, then the pastor will decide who will lead the service. There is a precedence for liturgical worship. Priests have first precedence; then deacons. If clergy are not available, the pastor may select a lay leader of prayer.

All liturgical ministers will need an outline of the service ahead of time and it might be necessary to schedule a rehearsal; especially if exposition does not usually take place in your parish.

---

22 See page 49.

Preparations

There are many items to keep in mind as you ready your liturgical spaces for exposition or other services in the presence of the Eucharist that are outside of Mass. As noted above, choose ministers to preside, read, serve, and sing. Light candles and have them ready around the altar or at the edges of the altar. Four to six candles should be used during exposition. Make sure you ready incense to be filled in the boat(s) that are used to hold the grains of incense. Thuribles should be cleaned ahead of time. Burnt incense can have a rotten or musty smell. Have charcoal, matches or lighters ready.

Depending on your liturgical space, have the monstrance ready, polished, cleaned, and available to move into its place on the altar. Some monstrances require their own matching luna. Make sure the humeral veil, alb, stole, and other needed liturgical garments have been cleaned, ironed, and pressed. Prepare the necessary worship aids, hymnals, presider's books or ritual binders, and mark the necessary pages in the Lectionary (or ritual binder if that is what is used for the readings). Rehearse with musicians ahead of time.

Last, some liturgical spaces will need a "throne" to elevate the monstrance if the setting is too distant or too low to allow the monstrance to be seen. This helps the assembly view the Blessed Sacrament. Sometimes better lighting helps. Keep the sanctuary well lit while using dimmer lighting over the assembly. This helps focus the assembly's attention upon the monstrance while providing enough light for them to see their worship aids or hymnals.

Liturgical Environment

The liturgical environment team must always take care to keep the emphasis upon devotional elements proportionately smaller than the emphasis on the liturgical elements. Decorating a separate chapel as you routinely decorate for the church assures that the chapel is "dressed" for the Rite of Exposition. If exposition takes place within the main church, there is no need to adapt the environment beyond what you would have done for the season or Sunday Mass. The Blessed Sacrament, exposed in the monstrance, should be the central focus. Adding floral arrangement or other items that are not usually in place will draw attention to themselves—and away from Christ whom we adore in the Blessed Sacrament.

As noted earlier, if the Sacrament is exposed in a monstrance, four to six candles are lighted and placed around the monstrance. The Sacrament is also incensed. However, if the Sacrament is exposed in a ciborium, the ritual book recommends that "at least two candles"[23] be used. Incense is encouraged but not required. This is similar to what happens at Mass, thus, ritually connecting the two celebrations.[24]

The rite is clear that only candles and the monstrance are placed upon the altar during exposition. Other liturgical norms for the environment should be considered as well with regards to the altar. For example, *Built of Living Stones* states: "The altar should remain clear and free-standing, not walled in by massive floral displays."[25] *Built of Living Stones* uses the Christmas crib as an example of something that would block the altar. Using this as guidance, it is best that other icons or statues of the saints not be placed around the altar. Saints lead us to Christ; however, no saintly image should obscure or take precedence over Christ's presence in the Rite of Exposition of the Blessed Sacrament.

Regulations and Norms

Before reviewing the order of service for the Rite of Exposition and Benediction, it is important to understand a few general regulations from *Holy Communion and Worship of the Eucharist Outside Mass* and the *Order for the Solemn Exposition of the Holy Eucharist.*

The ordinary minister for exposition is the priest or deacon. With permission from the local ordinary, a layperson may also "publicly expose and later repose"[26] the Eucharist. The layperson may open the tabernacle and place the host in the monstrance or place the ciborium upon the altar and then "replace the blessed sacrament in the tabernacle."[27] Only a priest or deacon may incense the Blessed Sacrament or bless the gathered assembly with the monstrance, or, offer benediction.

Ordained ministers may wear an alb, or a cassock with surplice and a stole. The color of the stole is either white or the color of the season or day.

---

23 See HCW, 85.

24 The GIRM notes, "The altar is to be covered with at least one white cloth. In addition, on or next to the altar are to be placed candlesticks with lighted candles: at least two in any celebration, or even four or six, especially for a Sunday Mass or a Holyday of Obligation, or if the Diocesan Bishop celebrates, then seven candlesticks with lighted candles" (117).

25 BLS, 124.

26 HCW, 91; see also OSE, 26.

27 HCW, 91; see also OSE, 26.

The ordained ministers will also use a humeral veil to hold the monstrance if the Eucharist is not reserved where exposition is taking place and a procession from the separate chapel to the main space is needed. For benediction, ordained ministers wear a white cope and a humeral veil to hold the monstrance. Lay ministers may wear an alb for exposition, depending on local custom. Lay ministers should not wear a humeral veil.[28]

The ritual distinguishes between "lengthy exposition" and a "brief period of exposition."[29] Places that reserve the Eucharist (parishes, shrines, religious communities, hospital chapels, campus ministry centers) should expose the Sacrament "for an extended period of time" at least "once a year."[30] This does not have to be continuous and it can be interrupted. The local ordinary must give permission for extended periods of exposition to take place and a "reasonable number of the faithful"[31] should be present.

A period of lengthy exposition may take place throughout the day or spread over several days, such as during a parish mission or Forty Hours,[32] or it may take place perpetually[33] (each day of the year). Usually, these longer periods are in parishes with larger amounts of people attending. How extended this period of exposition will be is dependent on whether the parish has sufficient numbers of people to pray in the presence of the Blessed Sacrament during the hours that the parish is advertising that exposition is taking place. If a parish does not have sufficient numbers of people to pray in the presence of the Blessed Sacrament, then the duration of exposition should be shortened so that sufficient numbers of people are present. The pastor or parish team may simply schedule one hour for exposition after the last Mass on Sunday to ensure that there will be a suitable number of people remaining in the Church to allow the parish to have exposition of the Blessed Sacrament.

In times of "serious and general need"[34] a bishop may request that parishes schedule longer periods of exposition, even in small parishes. This serious need is usually because of tragic situations or disastrous weather

---

28 The ritual notes that lay ministers should "wear either the liturgical vestments that are used in the region or the vesture that is befitting this ministry and is approved by the Ordinary" (HCW, 92; OSE, 27). The alb is usually the liturgical vesture worn by lay ministers in the United States.

29 See HCW, 86–89.

30 HCW, 86 and OSE, 11.

31 HCW, 86; see also OSE, 11. Extended periods of adoration may last for several hours, days, or even perpetually (24/7).

32 See page 44.

33 See page 41.

34 HCW, 87.

conditions. For example, many will recall that while the United States was suffering from the effects of the terroristic attacks on September 11, 2001, many bishops directed that local parishes offer exposition for longer periods. People needed to pray and turn to God to help them through a very difficult time.

For lengthy periods of exposition and benediction, the act of exposition itself (placing the host in the luna and then in the monstrance) should immediately follow Mass.

There are several options for other liturgical rites to take place during exposition, such as the Liturgy of the Hours,[35] Eucharistic services (or services of the Word),[36] and other variations of prayer.[37] These can be scheduled throughout the day or regularly if a parish offers perpetual exposition. Or, for short periods of exposition, a particular liturgical service may be done (for example, a one hour period of exposition with a service of the Word). Exposition may immediately follow Mass[38] or it may occur at a separate time.[39] However, during the period of exposition, Mass should not take place at the same time of exposition if exposition is taking place where Mass would ordinarily be celebrated. Exposition and Mass can occur simultaneously if exposition is taking place in a place separate from where Mass will be celebrated (such as the Blessed Sacrament chapel), providing that there are two people present in prayer in the presence of the Sacrament.[40] What follows is an explanation of the various rituals as provided in *Holy Communion and Worship of the Eucharist Outside Mass* and the *Order for the Solemn Exposition of the Holy Eucharist.*

Exposition after Mass

Exposition does not need to follow Mass; however, for a "more solemn and lengthy exposition" the host that is used should have been consecrated at a Mass "immediately" preceding the initial exposition.[41] *Holy Communion and Worship of the Eucharist Outside Mass* provides few details for how the ritual actually happens other than providing the norms for when Mass is required

---

35 See page 37.

36 See page 44.

37 See page 40.

38 See below.

39 See page 32.

40 See HCW, 83, OSE, 8, and the BCL Newsletter from June, 1995, which states: "Every effort should be made to ensure that there should be at least two people present. There must absolutely never be periods when the Blessed Sacrament is exposed and there is no one present for adoration."

41 HCW, 94.

to precede exposition. Parish staffs will need to consult the *Order for the Solemn Exposition of the Holy Eucharist* for this information. Although primarily published for Forty Hours, the rituals in this book can be used in other circumstances. Chapter 1 includes the "Opening Celebration of the Eucharist," which is meant to precede the Rite of Exposition. It serves as a good model for a Mass preceding exposition. Here is a basic order of service:

Liturgy of the Eucharist

- Preparation of the Gifts [gifts for the poor]
- Mass occurs as usual

Communion Rite at Mass [occurs as usual]

- Distribution of Holy Communion [both species]

Exposition

- Host is placed in the monstrance
- Prayer after Communion
- [Concluding Rites are omitted]
- Incensation and song
- Prayer
- [optional procession]
- [Period of adoration may occur here with Scripture, songs, prayers, and silence]

Benediction

A sacristan makes the "usual preparations"[42] that are made for Mass as well the items needed for exposition and benediction.

A host that fits the luna is prepared and placed with the larger host for Mass. These two special hosts are put in the paten, ciboria, or bowls filled with hosts and placed at the credence table before Mass. These patens, ciboria, or bowls will be brought forward during the Preparation of the Gifts. The luna and the monstrance may be placed on the side table in the sanctuary or kept in the sacristy.

The rite indicates that Mass is celebrated as usual until the Preparation of the Gifts. At that time, the rite recommends that gifts for the poor are brought forth. This situates the Mass and the devotion that follows with the social mission of the Church.

---

42 OSE, 28.

The rite also emphasizes that both species should be consecrated and given at Mass.[43]

During the Communion Rite, especially at the Sign of Peace, the altar server or the sacristan brings the luna forward and places it on the altar. If an older host has been in the luna from a previous time exposition service, it is broken and placed in the ciborium that is in the tabernacle. The priest places the host in the luna. The other host is shown to the assembly and broken as the Lamb of God is sung.

As the assembly receives Communion, the sacristan or altar server removes all the Mass items from the altar, except for the luna and corporal. Because exposition of the Blessed Sacrament follows Mass, the monstrance is brought from the side table or sacristy and brought forward to be placed on the altar while the faithful are receiving Communion. Once the distribution of Holy Communion is complete, the priest places the luna in the monstrance and turns the monstrance to face the assembly. The monstrance may be placed on a throne. The priest returns to the presidential chair.

The Prayer after Communion is recited at the chair. This prayer ends the Mass since the Concluding Rites are omitted. The Rite of Exposition continues either in the main worship space where Mass was celebrated, or a procession occurs moving the monstrance to a separate chapel.[44] The assembly may be invited to participate in this procession.

If exposition remains in the main worship space, exposition continues at the same altar that was used for Mass. The priest celebrant goes to the altar and the deacon or server brings the thurible to him. At that point he adds the incense. The priest kneels along with the congregation and incenses the Blessed Sacrament. Traditionally, "*O Salutaris*" or "*Tantum ergo*" is sung at this time, although, the rite simply says any "suitable song"[45] may be sung.

If exposition takes place in a separate chapel, the priest goes to the altar, picks up the monstrance (or possibly a small ciborium that may used for exposition in a small chapel with a small tabernacle); then there is a procession to the Blessed Sacrament chapel altar or tabernacle. A song may be sung during the procession.[46] An altar server or sacristan can lead the way to open

---

43 It is helpful to note that this ritual was published in 1993, and so the additional rubric, "additional wine may be consecrated in a flagon," is no longer in force. Wine may no longer be consecrated in a flagon (see RS, 106).

44 Or, as on the Solemnity of the Most Holy Body and Blood of Christ (*Corpus Christi*), a longer procession through the local community may take place. Refer to page 47.

45 See OSE, 35; see also STL, 243.

46 See OSE, 35.

the door(s) to the Blessed Sacrament chapel and the monstrance is placed on the altar. There should be a cloth on the altar, regardless if it is in the main worship space or separate chapel. The monstrance may be placed on a throne. The throne "should not be too lofty or distant."[47]

Again, as noted above, if exposition remains in the same place Mass was celebrated, after the monstrance is placed on the throne the deacon or server brings the thurible to the priest celebrant who adds incense. He kneels along with the congregation and incenses the Blessed Sacrament. Traditionally, "*O Salutaris*" or "*Tantum ergo*" is sung at this time, although, the rite simply says any "suitable song"[48] may be sung.

Exposition apart from Mass

If exposition takes place during a short period, it is not required that exposition takes place immediately following Mass (although it is not forbidden). Instead, particular times can be scheduled that are apart from Mass. For example, some parishes might wish to schedule exposition every Wednesday night during Lent. This might be for an hour after the workday or on Sunday evenings. It could be combined with a service of the Word or Evening Prayer.

Here is a basic order of service if Mass does not precede exposition (note that many alternatives or adaptations may be done). This outline presumes that the Blessed Sacrament has not been exposed prior to the beginning of the liturgy:[49]

Exposition

- Entrance of ministers
- Exposition
- Incensation and song
- Greeting
- Collect

---

47 HCW, 93 and OSE, 13.

48 OSE, 35; see also STL, 243.

49 The liturgical Rite of Exposition and Benediction does not only occur when the Blessed Sacrament has not been previously exposed. For those who have ongoing periods of exposition, there are several options of liturgical prayer taking place in the presence of the exposed Blessed Sacrament at different times of the day. If the sacrament is exposed, the ministers approach the altar, genuflect, and go directly to their chairs (see OSE, 105).

Adoration
- Liturgy of the Word
- Homily
- Intercessions
- Lord's Prayer

Benediction
- Incensation and song
- Prayer

Reposition [optional]
- Acclamation or song

A shorter period of exposition may take place in the main worship space or in a separate chapel. If the tabernacle is not located in the same space where the Rite of Exposition will take place, a procession with the Sacrament from the tabernacle to the place of reservation will need to occur.

When Mass does not precede exposition, the people gather in the place of exposition. The ministers approach the altar in silence or are accompanied by instrumental music. If the Eucharist has already been exposed and placed on the altar, the ministers should genuflect to the Sacrament and go to their chairs. If the Eucharist has not been exposed, the ministers process to the tabernacle to retrieve the Sacrament, bring it to the altar, and place it in the monstrance.[50] The ordained "minister puts on a humeral veil and brings the sacrament from the place of reservation."[51] Altar servers with lighted candles may accompany the ordained minister. The minister places the monstrance on a cloth-covered altar.

After the monstrance is placed on the altar, the ordained minister incenses the Sacrament, usually swinging the thurible three times to show reverence. All are invited to sing a Eucharistic-themed song. It is best to select a song that your assembly is familiar with. "Gift of Finest Wheat (You Satisfy the Hungry Heart)" or the traditional hymn, "*Tantum ergo*" are good options. After the incensation and the song, the ministers go to their chairs and the presider greets the faithful. A collect follows.

---

50 See for example, OSE, 38–39.
51 HCW, 93.

Adoration during Exposition

Regardless of how the Rite of Exposition and Benediction begins (either immediately following Mass or apart from Mass), a period of adoration follows the act of exposition.[52] When preparing this ritual, parish teams need to ensure that the gathered assembly is brought to full, conscious, and active participation. The ritual clearly calls for "prayers, songs, and readings to direct the attention of the faithful to the worship of Christ the Lord"[53] as well as a "homily or brief exhortations to develop a better understanding of the Eucharistic mystery."[54] Periods of silence are also encouraged.

Holy Communion and Worship of the Eucharist is vague about the exact order of the service other than to say it is to include readings, prayers, music, and silence. Chapter IV of the ritual offers suggestions for biblical texts as well as various antiphons, responsories, and prayers for benediction. This suggests that there is a great deal of flexibility involved with preparing this ritual for your parish.[55] Parishes may also refer to the *Order for the Solemn Exposition of the Holy Eucharist* for more detailed rubrics and options.[56]

The *Order for Solemn Exposition of the Holy Eucharist* provides two Eucharistic services that may be done during the period of adoration.[57] These Eucharistic services are essentially a Liturgy of the Word. They are designed to open exposition with a period of prayer, perhaps for a retreat, an evening reflection, or other time of prayer in the community's life. The presiding minister is normally a priest or a deacon, but a layperson, entrusted by the pastor, may lead the celebration in the absence of clergy.

Holy Communion and Worship of the Eucharist Outside Mass does not provide a particular sequence of readings; only that "one or more . . . Scripture readings are then read."[58] *The Order for the Solemn Exposition of the Holy Eucharist,* however, suggests particular Scripture texts but notes that others may be chosen as well. Readings may be chosen and placed in an order similar to the Liturgy of the Word at Mass, with a First Reading from the Old Testament followed by a Responsorial Psalm, a Second Reading from the

---

52 See HCW, 95–96.

53 HCW, 95.

54 HCW, 95.

55 For example, the Liturgy of the Hours may also be done instead of a service of the Word. Refer to page 37.

56 See page 21.

57 Please note that beginning of these services are outlined above (exposition after Mass or exposition without Mass).

58 OSE, 97.

New Testament, and a Gospel Acclamation followed by the Gospel. Suggested readings are provided in the ritual book. It is also preferred that opportunities for singing and silence are integrated in the service. Intercessions modeled on the format of the Universal Prayer at Mass may also be included. Note that during the intercessions, the assembly is invited to kneel.[59] Sample texts are provided in the ritual book.[60] The Lord's Prayer is also included before benediction is offered.

Based on what is included in the *Order for the Solemn Exposition of the Holy Eucharist*,[61] the following model for this period of prayer might be used during the period of adoration (the time frame is merely an estimate):

- First Reading from the Old Testament (2–3 minutes)
- Silence (5 minutes)
- Responsorial Psalm (3–5 minutes)
- Silence (5 minutes)
- Second Reading (2–3 minutes)
- Silence (5 minutes)
- Gospel Acclamation (1 minute)
- Gospel (2–3 minutes)
- Homily (5–7 minutes)
- Silence (5 minutes)
- Intercessions (3 minutes)
- Lord's Prayer
- Extended silence (optional)

The time frame for extended silence depends upon your parish's needs. Benediction might not immediately follow the period of adoration.[62] Instead, for an extended period of adoration during exposition, benediction might be at a later time in the day. Some parishes devote one day per month for exposition. On a "day of prayer," there are prolonged periods of silence

---

59 See OSE, 99.

60 See OSE, 99.

61 The explanation of the Eucharistic services or Liturgies of the Word is based on what is included in OSE, 91–116. Please note that this section of the ritual book includes suggestions for readings and texts for the prayers. The appendix in this ritual book provides Scripture readings for the different liturgical years (A, B, or C), litanies ("Litany of the Holy Eucharist," "Invocation of Christ"), prayers at benediction of the Blessed Sacrament, and suggested music.

62 See page 36 regarding benediction.

and benediction occurs at the end of the day (sometimes before dinner time, early evening, or around 7 PM). Conclude the day with Evening or Night Prayer, especially in communities that are already familiar with the Liturgy of the Hours. Benediction may be included.[63]

If there is an extended period of silence, those who pray will need to sign up for a time to pray at every hour until exposition concludes with benediction or reposition or both. When those who pray arrive for their assigned hour of prayer, it is best for them to pray communally with a reading, a short prayer, perhaps the Lord's Prayer, and maybe a song.[64]

Benediction

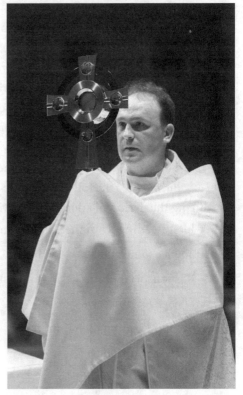

Benediction is the blessing of the assembly with the exposed sacrament.

Benediction occurs toward the end of the entire Rite of Exposition and is the official blessing that a priest or deacon gives with the exposed Sacrament. The rite is clear that exposition should not be offered "merely for the purpose of giving of benediction."[65] Benediction may occur daily for parishes that provide perpetual exposition.[66]

At the end of the period of adoration, the minister goes to the altar, genuflects, and kneels before the monstrance. In most places, the assembly joins with the presider in kneeling before the Blessed Sacrament. A Eucharistic hymn is sung. It has been the custom to sing "*Tantum ergo*" but other songs are appropriate, especially those that connect our Eucharistic theology to mission and service in the world. Good examples are "Bread for the World" by Bernadette Farrell, "*Ubi Caritas*" by Bob Hurd, or "Here at this Table" by Janet Sullivan Whitaker and Max Whitaker. Whatever songs are chosen,

---

63 See page 37 for pastoral suggestions for praying the Liturgy of the Hours in the presence of the Blessed Sacrament.

64 See page 41 for more details concerning perpetual exposition.

65 HCW, 89.

66 In these cases, reposition does not necessarily follow.

be sure that they are familiar to those present. While the song is sung, the minister incenses the Sacrament. After the incensation, the minister stands to say a brief prayer.[67]

After the prayer, the ordained minister "puts on the humeral veil, genuflects, and takes the monstrance. . . . He makes the sign of the cross over the people . . . in silence."[68] If a layperson presides, they are not to give benediction. Instead, a lay minister reposes the Blessed Sacrament.

Reposition

Reposition is the removal of the Blessed Sacrament from the monstrance and returning the Sacrament to the tabernacle. As stated above, if a layperson is presiding, they do not bless the faithful with the monstrance. Instead the lay presider genuflects (or possibly bows, depending on local custom) to the Blessed Sacrament, retrieves the luna, turns the monstrance slightly, and places the luna back in the tabernacle. After placing the Blessed Sacrament in the tabernacle, the lay presider genuflects (or possibly bows) before the Blessed Sacrament, and then closes the tabernacle doors.

If a priest or deacon is presiding, the Blessed Sacrament is reposed after benediction. While the Blessed Sacrament is being returned to the tabernacle, the assembly sings a song of praise. Songs familiar to your community such as "Holy God, We Praise Thy Name" or "God, We Praise You" are very appropriate. Some communities sing or say the Divine Praises; however, this is not part of the ritual text and is not required.[69]

Reposition occurs if a parish is offering a short period of exposition or if longer periods of exposition are interrupted (for example, Mass, Reconciliation services, or wedding rehearsals taking place in the church). In this latter case, reposition can only happen twice in one day.[70]

The Liturgy of the Hours during Exposition

As already mentioned, the Liturgy of the Hours may also be prayed during exposition. This is especially appropriate for periods of long exposition but it also might be done for a short period as well.

---

67 Prayers are found in HCW, 98. Other prayers from the OSE or even *The Roman Missal* may be used. See page 24.

68 HCW, 99.

69 See page 76.

70 See HCW, 88.

The Order for the Solemn Exposition of the Holy Eucharist includes three orders of Prayer for the Liturgy of the Hours: two services for Evening Prayer and one service for Morning Prayer. Morning Prayer and Evening Prayer are the important "hinges of prayer"[71] for the life of the Church, and it is the "duty of the church"[72] to pray these Hours. "The purpose of the liturgy of the hours is to sanctify the day and the whole range of human activity."[73] The Liturgy of the Hours is an excellent preparation for Eucharist[74] for the Hours "extends the praise and thanksgiving offered to God in the eucharistic celebration to the several hours of the day."[75]

It is part of the life of the Church to give praise to God at appropriate times of the day and the Liturgy of Hours has served as a model for centuries. Evening Prayer celebrated in the presence of the Blessed Sacrament is a way to extend the praise and thanksgiving to God.[76] The texts found in *The Order for the Solemn Exposition of the Holy Eucharist* are from the Solemnity of the Most Holy Body and Blood of Christ. However, parishes and religious communities are not bound to these texts and may substitute the prayers of the day from the Roman Office. The Liturgy of the Hours may be prayed if exposition is already occurring or the Sacrament may be exposed during the Hours. Here is the outline of exposition during Evening Prayer:

Exposition

- Entrance of the Ministers[77]
  - ▫ [Exposition: if Sacrament is not already exposed]
  - ▫ [Incensation and song]
- Introduction[78]
- Eucharistic hymn

---

71 See *General Instruction of the Liturgy of Hours* (GILOH), 29.

72 CSL, 85.

73 GILOH, 11.

74 See GILOH, 12.

75 HCW, 96.

76 See OSE, 37.

77 This follows the rubrics as described on page 32.

78 This is the regular opening verse from the Liturgy of the Hours, namely "O God, come to my assistance. Lord, make haste to help me. Glory to the Father . . . ," and so on.

Adoration

- Psalmody
  - Antiphon 1 and Psalm[79]
  - Antiphon 2 and Psalm
  - Antiphon 3 and New Testament Canticle
- Reading
- Homily
- Responsory
- Canticle of Mary
- Intercessions
- Lord's Prayer

Benediction (optional)

- Incensation and song
- Prayer

Reposition (optional)

- Acclamation or song (optional)

Closing Prayer

- Acclamation or song (optional)

Morning Prayer and the additional service for Evening Prayer follow the same model above (of course, the Canticle of Zechariah is sung at Morning Prayer and the Canticle of Mary is sung at Evening Prayer). For assistance with celebrating the Liturgy of Hours in your parish, please review the *General Instruction of the Liturgy of Hours.*

In parishes that have exposition of the Blessed Sacrament through the day (and maybe even through the night), it is strongly encouraged that the Liturgy of the Hours is celebrated in the presence of the Sacrament. *The Liturgy of Hours* ritual books (found in four volumes) may be available to encourage individual recitation or the communal praying of Morning, Midday, Evening, or Night Prayer liturgies. A simpler version is found in *Christian Prayer* or *Shorter Christian Prayer.* You may wish to encourage that your parish pray the Liturgy of the Hours before a meeting. Have all the parish

---

79 A sung or recited antiphon begins and ends the recitation or chanting of the psalms. Parishes might consult settings of the Responsorial Psalm as a simple way to sing the psalms.

organizations that meet at 7 PM, for example, gather in the chapel, where exposition is already occurring, and join in the "prayer of the church."[80]

Before leaving the chapel to go to a parish meeting, offer benediction. The ordained minister goes to the altar, genuflects or bows, kneels (if possible), and a Eucharistic song may be sung. Reposition is omitted since perpetual exposition is occurring.

If benediction does not occur during the Liturgy of the Hours, then Morning or Evening Prayer ends as usual, except the blessing and dismissal is omitted.[81] The parish volunteers leave the chapel to attend their meetings and other parishioners remain to continue praying in the chapel while the Blessed Sacrament is exposed.

Exposition of the Blessed Sacrament with Taizé Prayer

It is becoming popular to have Taizé prayer in the presence of the Blessed Sacrament. Taizé is a place in south-central France where an ecumenical community of vowed and nonvowed religious men and women live a common life of prayer and work. This community has developed a form of prayer (often incorporating the Liturgy of the Hours) using the Cross as a focal point, along with music, Scripture, and silence. One of the members of the Taizé community, Jacques Berthier,[82] composed a particular style of music to be used during their prayer. The music is performed as a mantra, singing a repeated refrain accompanied with the layering of harmonic voices and various instrumentation. This style of prayer can be used during exposition. The exposed Sacrament takes the place of the Cross as the central focus. Here is an example of exposition of the Blessed Sacrament in the style of Taizé:

- Entrance of the ministers and exposition of the Blessed Sacrament [incensation would occur as usual]
- Opening song (refrain is repeated for 3 minutes)
- Collect (1 minute)
- Silence (5 minutes)
- Song (refrain repeated for 3 minutes)
- Silence (5 minutes)

---

80 See GILOH, 5–33; see especially GILOH, 32.

81 See OSE, 85–90.

82 Jacques Berthier passed away in 1994. His music is available in the United States from GIA Publications, Inc. (www.giamusic.com).

- Reading (3 minutes)

- Silence (5 minutes)

- Song (5 minutes)

- Reading (2 minutes)

- Silence (5 minutes)

- Intercessions (2 minutes)

- Benediction [incensation would occur as usual]

- Song (3 minutes)

- Reposition

- Closing song or all depart in silence

Perpetual Exposition

Perpetual exposition is continuous prayer in the presence of the Blessed Sacrament exposed in the monstrance. In order for this to be offered continuously, it is best if this takes place in a separate chapel. *Built of Living Stones* provides practical guidelines for where this should take place:

> "Some parishes have inaugurated the practice of continuous adoration of the Eucharist. If, for some good reason, perpetual exposition must take place in a parish church, the Congregation for Divine Worship and the Discipline of the Sacraments has directed that this take place in a separate chapel that is 'distinct from the body of the church so as not to interfere with the normal activities of the parish or its daily liturgical celebration.'"[83]

When a parish, shrine, or other Catholic community is considering having perpetual exposition, it is necessary to receive permission from the local ordinary (the bishop) of a diocese. The parish will need to provide the bishop with evidence of a commitment of persons,[84] two for each hour of the day, and the particular plan for the local community for the benefit of this prayer.[85] In Scripture, Jesus said: "where two or three are gathered together

---

83 BLS, 78; referencing *Paschale solemnitatis* (PS), 49: "For the reservation of Blessed Sacrament, a place should be prepared and adorned in such a way as to be conducive to prayer and meditation; that sobriety appropriate to the liturgy of these days is enjoined, to the avoidance or suppression of all abuses."

84 HCW, 86.

85 These hours of prayer are called Holy Hours. Holy Hours may also occur in the presence of the Sacrament reserved in the tabernacle.

in my name, there am I in the midst of them."[86] This statement has been a traditional source for the requirement of having at least two people present. Having two people present also provides a "backup plan" should one of these persons is not able to attend as previously scheduled. This means a minimum of 336 people making a commitment for one week of around-the-clock prayer (24/7), plus extra people who will be available to substitute for those who may be ill or on holiday.

> For where two or three are gathered together in my name, there am I in the midst of them.
>
> —Matthew 18:20

If a parish is interested in offering perpetual exposition, it is advisable that the pastor and liturgical staff work with the pastoral council, liturgy committee, and other leaders of the community to obtain a sense of the time commitment from the parish. It will be helpful to create a "24/7 chart" to help members understand the hourly commitment and have volunteers fill in the hours to pray over the week (or month). Once the parish has made the commitment to cover the hours (or bands), a letter is written to the bishop requesting permission for extended periods of exposition.

When the parish initiates perpetual exposition, Mass should precede the Rite of Exposition.[87]

While the Eucharist is exposed, communal prayer should occur. Services can be scheduled at particular times, complete with liturgical ministers and music. However, this is not always possible—liturgies cannot occur 24/7. In order to ensure that each hour of prayer includes communal praying, encourage those who have signed up to pray the Lord's Prayer, recite a psalm, or sing a song when they arrive along with those who are completing their scheduled time of prayer. This practice is like the "passing of the prayer torch." *Holy Communion and Worship of the Eucharist Outside Mass* emphasizes that there should be communal prayer during the period of adoration:

"During the exposition there should be prayers, songs, and readings to direct the attention of the faithful to the worship of Christ the Lord.

"To encourage a prayerful spirit, there should be readings from Scripture with a homily or brief exhortations to develop a better understanding of the

---

86 Matthew 18:20.
87 See the explanation on page 29.

eucharistic mystery. It is also desirable for the people to respond to the word of God by singing and to spend some periods of time in religious silence."[88]

There is a great deal of flexibility with communal prayer during the period of adoration when the Blessed Sacrament is exposed. Many forms of prayer may be done.[89]

Periods of silence should be included. It is during this time that those who have gathered to pray may do whatever form of prayer that are comfortable with praying—novenas, the Rosary, meditation with Scripture, reading reflections on the Eucharist, or just talking silently to God.

At set times, the rituals from *Order for the Solemn Exposition of the Holy Eucharist* may be done.

As mentioned previously, when the Sacrament is exposed, at least two people must be present at all times. There is always cause for concern if someone does not show up for their scheduled time. Check with your pastor or pastoral minister who is responsible for your parish policy. In many parishes, when one of the people does not come for their assigned hour of prayer, the other person calls them to find out the reason (they may be sick, out of town, or forgot). They should then communicate the reason to the coordinator of exposition. If this becomes a habit, the person who is missing their assigned hour may be asked to take a break volunteering to pray in the presence of the Blessed Sacrament.

In general, when the person who is expected to pray does not appear because of some very good reason, someone is given permission by the pastoral leader of your parish to repose the Blessed Sacrament if it has been exposed in a monstrance or the tabernacle door is open. Laypersons may take the luna out of the monstrance and place the Blessed Sacrament in the tabernacle, genuflecting (or bowing) before closing the tabernacle door(s). Then one blows out the candles, retrieves the monstrance and the tabernacle key, and places them in a secure place, usually the sacristy.

The Eucharist must not be left unattended. If this happens, exposition must be interrupted and the Sacrament reposed. Therefore, if someone comes later in the day to pray in the presence of the Blessed Sacrament, they will find that the luna has been returned to the tabernacle and the monstrance and the tabernacle key are stored in the sacristy (or another appropriate place). People, of course, are free to pray in the church, chapel, or wherever the

---

88 HCW, 95.
89 See pages 24, 34, and 67.

Blessed Sacrament is reserved. It is permitted for the lay minister to reexpose the Eucharist in the tabernacle as long as the assigned people are present to pray in the presence of the Blessed Sacrament. However, reexposition may only occur twice in one day.

Forty Hours

Perpetual exposition does not need to be 24/7. Instead, it can be for a full day, or over a period of several days. Instead, some parishes offer the Forty Hours devotion. This may or may not be actually forty hours—however, it is often scheduled during a retreat or parish mission. Members of the parish gather and participate in Mass and exposition, and hear preaching or or other talks that encourage the faithful to live a Eucharistic life and to receive Holy Communion. The Sacrament of Penance may be offered. Some persons might gather and pray all night long in vigil. The hours of praying culminate with Mass or benediction.

The *Order for the Solemn Exposition of the Holy Eucharist* provides the rituals that parishes might consider using or adapting for Forty Hours: the opening and closing Mass or service, and the Liturgy of the Hours and Eucharistic services which can be scheduled at set times during the period of Forty Hours.[90]

The opening Mass may be celebrated as explained on pages 29–32. At the closing celebration (Mass), the Eucharist should be reposed in the tabernacle before Mass begins[91] because Mass cannot occur while the Sacrament is exposed. The Mass takes place as usual; however, the Sacrament will be reexposed at the end of the celebration and follows what is explained on pages 29–32. The service concludes with the Eucharistic blessing (benediction) and the Sacrament is reposed.

The *Order for Solemn Exposition of the Blessed Sacrament* also includes the option of having a closing celebration outside of Mass. It is essentially a Liturgy of the Word with a period of praise and intercession. Here is the outline of the rite:

Exposition

- Entrance of the Ministers
- [Exposition]

---

90 See pages 22–25.
91 See OSE, 121.

- [Incensation and song]
- Greeting
- Collect

Adoration (with Liturgy of the Word)
- First Reading
- Responsorial Psalm
- Second Reading
- Gospel Acclamation
- Gospel
- Homily
- Praise and Intercession
- Incensation and song
- Silent Prayer
- Intercessions or litany
- [optional procession]
- Prayer

Benediction

Reposition
- Acclamation or song

Perpetual Adoration

Perpetual exposition can be a rich part of our parish prayer life, but there are some circumstances when exposition simply may not work. Prayer in the presence of the Blessed Sacrament reserved in the tabernacle is certainly part of Catholic tradition and to be encouraged. Opportunities for this form of prayer might involve extending the invitation to parishioners to pray before the tabernacle constantly in perpetual adoration. It would seem that many people still think of "adoration" and "exposition" as the same thing or use the words interchangeably. "The Blessed Sacrament may be adored while contained in the tabernacle for an extended period of time; this is called 'perpetual adoration.'"[92]

---

92 *Thirty-One Questions on Adoration of the Blessed Sacrament*, 19.

Good catechesis and a thought-out plan is important if perpetual adoration is to be implemented in a parish. It is important to create a crew of dedicated core volunteers, and a start-up campaign with sign-up opportunities. Using today's technology could also make this easier by employing an online program like "SignUpGenius" or "VolunteerSpot" to recruit en masse; a social media page, an e-mail list to request substitutes, or a group-call program to text or pass on immediate needs could also prove helpful.

If the parish has a Eucharistic chapel with a separate, secure entrance with a keypad code for the safety of those taking evening and night shifts, this longer, continuous adoration is appropriate and easier to accomplish. If the tabernacle is located directly in the sanctuary, then continuous adoration might not be feasible, as adoration would surely be suspended while Mass takes place. Sometimes it is also difficult if there are other events scheduled within the church, such as weddings and funerals, choir practice, or other prayer services. One can pray while these are happening, but it may not be desirable to either those adoring before the tabernacle, or those involved in other events in the church. Similarly, because the Eucharist is removed from the tabernacle during the Sacred Paschal Triduum (except for the period of adoration immediately following the Evening Mass of the Lord's Supper), prayer in the presence of the Blessed Sacrament would not be possible at this time.

But this raises the question: if the Blessed Sacrament is reserved in the tabernacle, is there truly a need for sign-in times, or a structured adoration program? During periods of exposition it is required to have two people present at all times, but is this actually necessary for perpetual adoration when the Sacrament is reserved (not exposed) in the tabernacle? It seems that this might be more feasible for a concentrated effort for a shorter period, for example, if a parish decides to pray for a specific need during a particular month (such as Respect Life Month in October or for our dearly departed during November). It may also be needed if the church is located in a crime-filled area and the church needs to be locked.

In many churches, there is no organized or official "perpetual adoration" but parishioners often spend time in prayer by the tabernacle. Many pastors encourage parishioners to pray in the presence of the Blessed Sacrament. People may wish to take a few minutes before or after Mass with the Blessed Sacrament, or other may wish to stop in throughout the day. They may pray their Rosaries, Breviary, prayer books, read the Sacred Scriptures, or contemplate God in silence.

It is always amazing to witness the steady flow of traffic in the presence of the Blessed Sacrament each day: the businessman who spends his lunch hour in prayer, the school secretary who stops faithfully after work, and the regular meeting of an elderly widow and widower who meet and pray the Rosary aloud and say their prayers together in a tender fashion for their departed spouses.

Besides these individual moments in the presence of the Blessed Sacrament, the possibility for group prayer is unlimited. Perhaps parish groups can come before the tabernacle to pray the Divine Mercy Chaplet, Rosary, or the Liturgy of the Hours. Others may gather to pray for vocations and an end to abortion; to support a parish project, or to offer a novena for a special need.

Whether it is an organized team of prayers covering a particular hour of the week, encouraging people to spontaneously spend time in private prayer, or a regular group that meets at particular times in the presence of the Blessed Sacrament, adoration is surely encouraged so that we may draw closer to God, pray for all those in need of prayer, and pray for the world. As Pope Benedict XVI stated:

> "In the Eucharist, the Son of God comes to meet us and desires to become one with us; eucharistic adoration is simply the natural consequence of the eucharistic celebration, which is itself the Church's supreme act of adoration. Receiving the Eucharist means adoring him whom we receive. Only in this way do we become one with him, and are we given, as it were, a foretaste of the beauty of the heavenly liturgy. The act of adoration outside Mass prolongs and intensifies all that takes place during the liturgical celebration itself."[93]

Eucharistic Processions

Eucharistic processions literally take our Catholic faith to the streets. After Communion, the priest or deacon exposes the Blessed Sacrament in the monstrance. Then, with prayers and songs, the faithful leave the church and move into the neighborhood. The procession concludes with benediction. We do a Eucharistic procession on Holy Thursday when we transfer the

---

93 SacCar, 66.

Eucharist from a ciborium (or other vessel) from the main altar after Communion to the altar of repose, and there is the annual procession on the Solemnity of the Most Holy Body and Blood of Christ (*Corpus Christi*)[94] after the principal Mass.[95] The Eucharistic procession is a wonderful image of the journey God's people make in the company of the Risen Christ. Taking place either inside the church, around the church grounds, or from one parish to another, it is a strong witness to the whole neighborhood of our faith in the Eucharist. We pray that our homes, our streets, and our community may be blessed with Christ's presence.

Pope Benedict XVI spoke eloquently about the meaning of the procession for contemporary Catholics in his homilies for the Solemnity of the Most Holy Body and Blood of Christ (*Corpus Christi*). The procession is a profession of faith: this solemnity developed at a time when Catholics were both affirming and defining their faith "in Jesus Christ, alive and truly present in the Most Holy Sacrament of the Eucharist,"[96] and the procession is a public statement of that belief. But there is more. Benedict's statements emphasize the link with another Eucharistic procession—that of the Evening Mass of the Lord's Supper on Holy Thursday, where the Blessed Sacrament is borne from the main altar to the altar of repose. On *Corpus Christi,* "the church relives the mystery of Holy Thursday in the light of the Resurrection."[97] No longer walking with Jesus to the garden of Gethsemane, now we are following the Risen Lord who "goes ahead . . . to Galilee" (Matthew 28:7). Thus, the procession with the Blessed Sacrament has an evangelizing moment—taking the Gospel to the world in obedience to Christ's great commission.

At the same time, though, the procession is not just for Catholics. The mystery of the Eucharist is for everyone. The Sacrament of the Lord's Body and Blood always "goes above and beyond the walls of our churches."[98] Christ gives himself for us, but not *just* for us. The procession is a tangible realization of this, for as we go beyond our church walls, "we walk with the Risen One in his journey to meet the entire world."[99] The procession blurs the separa-

---

94 In the United States, this solemnity always occurs two Sundays after Pentecost.

95 Although the various ritual books specifically mention this solemnity as a time for the procession, processions may also occur after Mass at any time of the year with the bishop's permission as well as at the end of a "lengthy period of public adoration" (HCW, 103).

96 Homily of His Holiness Benedict XVI, Thursday, June 7, 2007. http://w2.vatican.va/content /benedict-xvi/en/homilies/2007/documents/hf_ben-xvi_hom_20070607_corpus-christi.html.

97 Homily of His Holiness Benedict XVI, Thursday, May 26, 2005. http://w2.vatican.va/content /benedict-xvi/en/homilies/2005/documents/hf_ben-xvi_hom_20050526_corpus-domini.html.

98Homily of His Holiness Benedict XVI, Thursday, May 26, 2006.

99 Homily of His Holiness Benedict XVI, Thursday, May 26, 2006.

tion between what we do inside the church and what we do outside: we "immerse [Christ], so to speak, in the daily routine of our lives, so that he may walk where we walk and live where we live."[100]

As we move from inside to outside, we must also move from an "insider mentality" to an awareness that Christ is for everyone. "The procession represents an immense and public blessing for our city."[101] To process is to go forward, and thus the procession speaks of the possibility of change, of transformation in Christ, for ourselves, our Church, and our world. The Eucharistic procession helps us recognize who we are as a Catholic community, and points us toward solidarity with others: "Those who recognize [Christ] in the sacred Host, recognize him in their suffering brother or sister."[102] Walking with Christ in the procession, we can see ourselves as members of his Body, but we can also look at the world through the loving eyes of Christ.

> In processions in which the eucharist is carried through the streets solemnly with singing, the Christian people give public witness to faith and to their devotion toward this sacrament.
>
> —*Holy Communion and Worship of the Eucharist Outside Mass,* 101

Preparing the Procession

When preparing the procession, parish teams may consult *Holy Communion and Worship of the Eucharist Outside Mass,* the *Ceremonial of Bishops,*[103] and *The Roman Missal.* However, the liturgical books offer surprisingly little guidance on how the procession should be carried out.

The rubrics for the Solemnity of the Most Holy Body and Blood of Christ (*Corpus Christi*) as found in *The Roman Missal* note the Church's preference for including a procession after Mass, but offer few other details:

> "It is desirable that a procession take place after the Mass in which the Host to be carried in the procession is consecrated. . . . If a procession takes place after mass, when the Communion of the faithful is over, the Concluding Rites are omitted and the procession forms."[104]

---

100 Homily of His Holiness Benedict XVI, Thursday, June 7, 2007.

101 Homily of His Holiness Benedict XVI, Thursday, May 26, 2006.

102 Homily of His Holiness Benedict XVI, Thursday, June 23, 2011. http://w2.vatican.va/content/benedict-xvi/en/homilies/2011/documents/hf_ben-xvi_hom_20110623_corpus-domini.html.

103 Although this collection of rubrics pertains to celebrations in which a bishop presides, the rubrics can be applied to usual parish practice. It includes many of the directives found in HCW. Cross-referencing is noted in the following additional footnotes.

104 See the rubrics in *The Roman Missal* for the Solemnity of the Most Holy Body and Blood of Christ (*Corpus Christi*).

This is useful information, of course, but a few things are missing: how to organize the procession, where to go, and what to do when you get there!

Fortunately, *Holy Communion and Worship of the Eucharist Outside Mass* and the *Ceremonial of Bishops* fill in a few of the blanks. If the procession immediately follows the end of Mass,[105] the celebrant (bishop or priest) may wear the chasuble or cope; if a lengthy period of adoration has intervened, then the cope is the proper vesture.[106] Following the Prayer after Communion, the celebrant adds incense to the thurible, goes to the altar, kneels, and incenses the Blessed Sacrament. Then he receives the humeral veil and picks up the monstrance. The *Ceremonial of Bishops* indicates the order for the procession—the crossbearer, accompanied by candle bearers, leads the way, but the thurifer does not walk in front of the cross as usual; rather, as on Holy Thursday,[107] two thurifers come immediately before the bishop (or priest) carrying the Blessed Sacrament. A baldachin (canopy) may be carried over the priest if desired, especially during poor weather conditions. The *Ceremonial of Bishops* also notes that "all carry candles, and torch-bearers escort the blessed sacrament."[108]

One significant element is missing from this description of the procession: the faithful! The *Ceremonial of Bishops* simply states,

> "The procession should be arranged in accordance with local custom in regard to the decoration of the streets and the order to be followed by the faithful who take part."[109]

Thus, there is room for—in fact, a need for—a fair amount of creativity in arranging the procession. The makeup of your parish community, the location of your church, and even the layout of the sanctuary will all have an impact on how the procession happens in your community. One thing is certain: the procession can happen in just about any community, large or small, urban or rural.

The rubrics offer some recommendations regarding the length of the procession, but no hard-and-fast guidelines:

---

105 The rubrics detailed above regarding Mass if followed by exposition should be observed. See page 29.

106 See *Ceremonial of Bishops* (CB), 390; HCW, 101-102. Other priests are encouraged to take part in the procession, even if they did not concelebrate. They may also wear a cope over a cassock and surplice (see CB, 390).

107 See page 55.

108 CB, 391.

109 CB, 392; HCW, 104.

"'There may be stations where eucharistic benediction is given, if there is such a custom and some pastoral advantage recommends it . . . it is fitting that the procession go from one church to another. But, when local circumstances require, the procession may return to the church where it began."[110] The rite specifies only that "at the end of the procession, eucharistic benediction is given in the church where the procession ends or in some other suitable place."[111]

The *Corpus Christi* procession is definitely not a "one-size-fits-all" occasion. Inner-city parishes may be able to walk to another nearby church or chapel, but in more suburban settings, the route might make a loop, moving around the block or around several blocks, and ending back at the church or in an outdoor gathering area.

If you have not done the procession before, keep it short and simple. The procession does not need to be miles long (or even many blocks) to be profoundly meaningful. Evaluate the

A procession with the Blessed Sacrament in the streets of Chicago. The procession is a witness of belief in the Real Presence of Christ in the Eucharist.

route each year. Does it speak to the full meaning of this public statement of faith? Or does it "play it safe," perhaps staying too close to home? Before you decide, be sure to investigate what is allowed for public gatherings in your area. Your local police department should be able to point you in the right direction.

Pacing the procession can be a challenge. With very long processions, a sharp turn, a step down or up, or any small distraction can create gaps that can make a procession not feel like a procession. Make sure the route is fairly level and accessible to all. The leaders (the crossbearer and candle bearers, perhaps escorted by someone specifically designated to know the route and set the pace) should walk very slowly. A slow, steady pace will help the rest of the procession stay tight and together, which in turn encourages participation

110 CB, 392–393; HCW, 104 and 107.
111 CB, 394.

in the spoken and sung responses along the way—people are less likely to participate if they are strung out in ones and twos. Another help in keeping the procession together is to have leaders with walkie-talkies or cell phones spaced through the procession, and able to communicate discreetly if problems arise. If large gaps form, the head of the procession can slow down or even stop for a few moments until the gap closes. Careful organization will help.

A slow, steady pace will help the rest of the procession stay tight and together.

The ritual books recommend music and prayer during the procession: "Songs and prayers should be planned for the purpose of expressing the faith of the participants and keeping their attention centered on the Lord alone."[112] Any time you have music outdoors it is a challenge, and if the procession is lengthy, the distance can make it even more difficult for all to sing together. It works well to have multiple musical groups spaced through the procession. Each of these groups should have the same repertoire of two or three chants which they will sing confidently, not trying to stay in time with every other group in the procession but simply encouraging the faithful who are walking nearest them to join in.

The best music for the procession are simple refrains that the community knows well without the need for a worship aid. The Litany of Saints, the Litany of the Sacred Heart of Jesus, or the Litany of the Most Holy Eucharist are simple to sing and can be extended or repeated if needed, making them ideal for a procession. Some contemporary music can work well, especially the chants of the Taizé community, which can be repeated over and over—"*Ubi Caritas*," "Jesus your Light," and "Jesus, Remember Me" are a few examples. You might "rehearse" one or two of these chants by using them as the Communion song at Mass in the weeks leading up to *Corpus Christi*, so that they can be sung with ease during the procession.

Spoken prayers can be used in addition to or in alternation with singing. The Rosary or the Divine Mercy Chaplet can easily be prayed from

---

112 CB, 392; HCW, 104.

memory. If you involve different ministry groups, each group might be encouraged to designate a prayer leader to select a prayer, and to lead those near them in prayer whenever the group is not singing. The end result will be a glad mix of song and spoken prayer.

In addition to the procession itself, and the sung and spoken prayers, there are other ways to participate. Children could carry small Eucharistic banners that they made in school or during religious education classes for this special occasion. Alternately, bells or colored streamers can be used, and adults can carry flowers or banners.

Depending on the length of the procession, you may stop once or several times for benediction of the Blessed Sacrament. The order is simple: the monstrance is set down on a temporary altar; a period of silence follows; then benediction is given, following the order laid out in *Holy Communion and Worship of the Eucharist Outside Mass* and the *Order for Solemn Exposition of the Holy Eucharist.* Then the procession continues to the next station, where benediction is given again, or back to the church.

When all the ministers enter the church they "go directly to their places"[113] in the sanctuary, the celebrant goes to the altar and, if there is a deacon, he takes the monstrance from the celebrant and places it on the altar. The celebrant and the deacon genuflect, the humeral veil is laid aside, and they both kneel before the altar. At this time, the deacon gives the thurible to the celebrant, both bow, and incense the Blessed Sacrament with three swings of the thurible. While the Sacrament is incensed, the assembly sings a Eucharistic song. The *Ceremonial of Bishops* recommends "*Tantum ergo.*" They bow to the Blessed Sacrament once more and the celebrant gives the incense back to the deacon.

Members of your parish environment team may decorate outdoor altars or stations.

The celebrant invites the assembly to pray with the invitation "Let us pray." Be sure to give some time for silent prayer. The prayer that follows may

---

113 CB,394.

be taken from *Holy Communion and Worship of the Eucharist Outside Mass* or the *Order for the Solemn Exposition of the Eucharist.*

After the final prayer, the celebrant takes the humeral veil and genuflects before the altar. The deacon may assist him with raising the monstrance before the people, and, performing the benediction, he makes the Sign of the Cross with the monstrance. The celebration should hold the monstrance with the humeral veil. Benediction is done in silence. The deacon takes the monstrance and places it on the altar, and he and the celebrant genuflect. The celebrant continues to kneel, and the deacon reposes the Sacrament to the place of reservation. After the silent benediction, the assembly may sing an acclamation.[114]

For a successful procession, some advanced preparations are necessary. The *Ceremonial of Bishops* specifies that before Mass, monstrance, humeral veil, host needed for the procession, and a second thurible with the boat of incense will need to be placed on the table in the sanctuary. And in another place easily accessible, the cope, torches, candles, and baldachin should be readied.[115] The parish will need catechesis. Even if you have done the procession for years—perhaps especially if you have "always done it"—provide some background on the origin and meaning of the solemnity in the bulletin or in homilies in the weeks preceding the *Corpus Christi* celebration. We cannot reiterate too many times what the procession is about, because, as the passages quoted above from Pope Benedict's homilies reflect, it has many dimensions. It is about faith in the Real Presence; it is about service of others; it is about who we are as Catholics; it is about Christ meeting the whole world. Provide clear communication on practical matters as well. Tell people in advance when the procession will occur, where it will go, and (for some the most important detail of all) how long it will take.[116] Help people know that their presence and participation matter.

Encourage parish councils and ministries to participate as groups. For instance, the children who have made their First Communion (wearing their finery again), candidates for Confirmation (perhaps wearing red), neophytes baptized at the Easter Vigil (perhaps wearing white) or catechumens and candidates in the ongoing process of the Rite of Christian Initiation of Adults,

---

114 See CB, 394.

115 See CB, 398.

116 LTP has prepared a resource for parishes to use in bulletins or upload to the parish website. It may be downloaded for free from this website: http://www.pastoralliturgy.org/resources/1005Repro Rsrc.pdf.

social outreach volunteers, Catholic school children and Knights of Columbus in their uniforms, Catholic Daughters of America, catechists, liturgical ministers—the list can go on. The procession is, of course, for the entire assembly, and should not be thought of as a series of special groups—but inviting such groups to join in can foster participation in the procession. Space these groups throughout the procession, not all in one place. In this way, their presence can help give shape to the procession.

Also beforehand, remember to contact the local police department for assistance with planning the route and providing help for traffic needs. The local media, social networks, and parish bulletin(s) would be a great place to advertise. Start with your biggest attendance events (Easter and Mother's Day) to raise awareness of this dynamic event in the life and history of our Church.

The Transfer of the Most Blessed Sacrament on Holy Thursday

The Evening Mass of the Lord's Supper concludes with one of the most important Eucharistic processions of the liturgical year. Following the Prayer after Communion, the priest celebrant carries the ciborium with the consecrated hosts in procession from the principal altar of the church to a "place of repose"[117] where it will remain, enclosed in a tabernacle, for solemn adoration until midnight.

It is altogether fitting to observe a special time of adoration on Holy Thursday, the day when we recall the institution of the Eucharist. But the transfer of the Most Blessed Sacrament has as much to do with Good Friday as it does with Holy Thursday. On Good Friday, the one day of the year when there is no Mass, Communion is given from hosts consecrated on Holy Thursday. These are the hosts carried in procession to the place of repose on Holy Thursday. So important is this link that in churches where the celebration of the Lord's Passion on Good Friday does not take place, the transfer of the Blessed Sacrament is not permitted.

The Roman Missal includes instructions for how the transfer is to take place, while the *Ceremonial of Bishops* provides additional detail. After Holy Communion, the ciborium containing the hosts to be distributed on Good Friday is left on the altar. After the Prayer after Communion, the celebrant

---

117 See the rubrics for Holy Thursday in *The Roman Missal*, 38.

goes to the altar with the thurifer, adds incense to the thurible, and, kneeling, incenses the ciborium. Then another server places the humeral veil around his shoulders, after which the celebrant picks up the ciborium and the procession to the place of repose begins. The procession is led by a crossbearer and two candle bearers. Others may follow, carrying lighted candles. These can be additional altar servers or other lay ministers—the choir, the readers, or perhaps the extraordinary ministers of Holy Communion. Then comes one or two[118] servers with lit thuribles and then the celebrant, carrying the ciborium, now covered in the humeral veil. Additional candles are carried immediately before and behind the celebrant.[119]

The procession moves from the primary altar of the church to the place of repose. This can be another part of the church, a separate chapel, or another space prepared for adoration. The key element is that the Blessed Sacrament *not* be placed in a tabernacle located at the main altar of the church, which is to be stripped after the Holy Thursday Mass. Thus, if your church has a

separate Blessed Sacrament chapel away from the main altar, it is appropriate to use this as the place of repose.[120] However, if the tabernacle is located at the main altar, or if the separate chapel is quite small, a separate place of repose will need to be established. The key elements will be a dignified place where a secure and worthy tabernacle can be placed for the period

The procession moves from the main altar to the altar of repose.

of adoration; sufficient seating for people to be able to come and spend time in the presence of the Blessed Sacrament; places for kneeling (even if the chairs do not have kneelers, several smaller kneelers or prie-dieux can be placed near the tabernacle for the use of the clergy in the procession and of others during the time of adoration); and some decorations. *The Roman*

118 While *The Roman Missal* mentions just one thurible, the *Ceremonial of Bishops* specifies two (see CB, 307).

119 "Around the blessed sacrament torches are carried" (CB, 307).

120 See PS, 49.

Missal indicates that the place of repose should be "suitably decorated"[121]: enhance the space with green plants, flowers, and lighted candles without going overboard and anticipating the full joy of Easter. Be sure parishioners and visitors can easily find the place of repose in your parish. Many Catholics observe the old custom of visiting several churches on the evening of Holy Thursday, and praying at the place of repose in each one. Make the procession route clear and simple enough that spoken instructions need not disrupt the end of the Evening Mass of the Lord's Supper. If instructions are needed, include them in the worship aid instead. If the place of repose is in a building separate from the church, be sure to provide signage on the church campus.

Music accompanies the procession during the transfer of the Most Blessed Sacrament. Any Eucharistic hymn can be sung, but the custom is to sing "*Pange lingua*," attributed to St. Thomas Aquinas. When "*Pange lingua*" is sung, the last two verses (beginning "*Tantum ergo*" and "*Genitori, genitoque*") are not sung until the very end of the procession, as the celebrant reaches the place of repose.

Upon arrival at the place of repose, the celebrant (or deacon, if there is one) places the ciborium in the tabernacle, leaving the doors open. Then the celebrant once again adds incense to the thurible and incenses the ciborium. The tabernacle is then closed. It remains closed for the entire period of adoration: exposition, whether in the ciborium or in a monstrance, is forbidden on Holy Thursday. At the conclusion of the song, the ministers remain for a time of adoration in silence, and then return to the sacristy without an elaborate procession.

Adoration of the Blessed Sacrament then continues until midnight. This can take place in silence, or there can be music or spoken prayer during this time. Night Prayer may be prayed at some point during the night, perhaps just before the conclusion of solemn adoration at midnight. Parishes might also consider incorporating a reading of the Gospel according to John, chapters 13–17, during the time of adoration.[122] These chapters take us from the Gospel of the Evening Mass of the Lord's Supper (the washing of the feet) through Judas' betrayal (the Last Supper discourses of Jesus and the high priestly prayer of John 17). A chapter might be read at the beginning of each hour of adoration.

---

121 See the rubrics for Holy Thursday in *The Roman Missal*, 38.
122 See PS, 56.

A decorated altar of repose for the transfer of the Holy Eucharist.

The period of solemn adoration ends at midnight. Adoration may continue after but "the adoration should be made without external solemnity, for the day of the Lord's Passion has begun."[123] In other words, if adoration is extended into the night, it needs to be simply in silence, without music or communal prayer.

Eucharistic Congresses

A form of Eucharistic devotion outside of Mass that may or may not be familiar to parishes is a Eucharistic congress. A Eucharistic congress provides a unique opportunity for the Christian faithful to gather together at an organized event to study about the Eucharist and to pray together. Usually, there are presentations about the Eucharist, Mass, opportunities for exposition, Eucharistic processions, and other Eucharistic devotions. They are held internationally and locally. Anyone can attend a Eucharistic congress.

International congresses are publicized on the Vatican website and elsewhere as part of the Roman Curia's Pontifical Committee for International Eucharistic Congresses. Every four years (as the current rotation has continued in the twenty-first century), the committee chooses a site so that the

---

123 See PS, 56.

world may gather for this retreat week devoted, as the committee says, to make better known, and to love and serve our Eucharistic Lord.

These events rotate around the globe and various cities and dioceses bid to host this multicultural, event. Over a week, participants join in Mass, talks, special rituals, processions, meals, and other social events to build understanding around the Eucharist. It is a special time of retreat and reflection, on the theology and practice of the Eucharist.

Until the pontificate of Pope John Paul II, the popes have attended very few International Eucharistic Congresses. Today, the pope often sends a delegate with a recorded address, which is presented during the final Mass of the congress. The address announces the site of the next host city.

The Archdiocese of Atlanta sponsors a Eucharistic congress each year. It began in 1996 as part of an attempt to renew Catholics' faith in the Eucharist, and offers a variety of speakers, workshops, and prayer opportunities.[124] These events incorporate the Eucharistic rituals as found in *Holy Communion and Worship of the Eucharist Outside Mass.*

> As a special manifestation of eucharistic worship . . . the purpose is that together the members of the Church join in the deepest profession of some aspect of the eucharistic mystery and express their worship publically in the bond of charity and unity.
>
> —*Holy Communion and Worship of the Eucharist Outside Mass,* 109

Parish Involvement

Since Eucharistic congresses are most often held on the diocesan or international level, it might not be clear how these events affect local parishes. Congresses are open to all the faithful, and parishioners should be encouraged to attend. The following ideas will help connect the larger diocesan (or international) event to the local parish:

- Advertise and promote any local or international events to parishioners in the bulletin and on the parish website, as well as include short explanations about the many dimensions of Catholic Eucharistic theology and how we worship the Eucharist both during and outside of Mass.

---

124 See the annual Eucharistic Congress website of the Archdiocese of Atlanta, http://congress.archatl.com/ as well as their Facebook page, www.facebook.com/econgress.atl. See also the website for the 51st International Eucharistic Congress taking place in the Philippines in January 2016, http://iec2016.ph/. Watch this YouTube video of the official theme song for this congress, www.youtube.com/watch?v=OJTxMOAmJNM.

- Host a number of opportunities such as various workshops or reflection days (either for the whole parish or for parishes in the deanery or vicariate).

- Offer opportunities for exposition.

- Host a parish potluck supper followed by a Eucharistic-themed film such as *Babette's Feast, Entertaining Angels,* or a documentary such as LTP's *A History of the Mass.* Parishioners can be encouraged to bring foods representing the diverse cultures—the diverse Body of Christ—in the parish. Provide time for small group discussions.

- Encourage families to eat meals together and provide supplemental catechesis about the Eucharist as meal.

- Provide families with resources to connect Sunday and the celebration of the Eucharist to their daily lives, such as LTP's *Celebrating Sunday for Catholic Families.*

- Organize a bread-baking party for teens, and bring this food to shut-ins or schedule volunteer opportunities at the local soup kitchen. When reflecting on the experience, be sure to link the social mission of the Church with the Eucharist. Show *Entertaining Angels,* a Eucharistic-themed movie about the life of Dorothy Day.

- Catholic school children might take part in an essay contest answering the question, "What does receiving the Eucharist mean to you?"

- At Sunday Mass, following the Prayer after Communion, neophytes can be invited to share a testimony or witness about coming to the Lord's Table. If your local congress is promoting a theme song, incorporate this song (providing it is liturgically appropriate) at Sunday Mass.

- Diocesan Congresses might form a joint choir, with representatives from the diocesan parishes serving as choir members, cantors, and instrumentalists. Invite your parish music ministry to take part!

Conclusion

Guide for Celebrating® Worship of the Eucharist Outside Mass has provided you with a broad and unique overview of the history of Catholic Eucharistic piety and how this has been expressed over the centuries and in our current, post-Conciliar Church. The pastoral advice will help you organize, celebrate, and gather your parishioners together to celebrate the various liturgies and devotional practices surrounding the heart of the Church, the Eucharist. These sections have woven a tapestry around the Eucharist to see that what we celebrate at Mass may be extended into the fruits of contemplative prayer in the Real Presence of our Risen Lord. May you stay and wait for the Lord in vigil, knowing that you are deepening and forming yourself into a Eucharistic union, assisting the Body of Christ to grow. As St. Peter Julian Eymard writes:

> "May you receive what you believe, be what you see, and continue to be formed in the gift of Christ's self until Christ's Eucharistic reign comes!"[125]

---

125 Translated into English from French by the private works of Fr. Hervé Thibault, sss, *Retreat Notes of Father Eymard*, Highland Heights, Ohio: Congregation of the Blessed Sacrament, 1988.

Frequently Asked Questions

Questions from Parish Staff

The following questions concern the preparation for prayer in the presence of the Blessed Sacrament that is outside of Mass.

1. ## What is the difference between liturgy and devotion? How are they are related? How are they separate? Do the liturgical rites of Eucharistic worship outside Mass involve devotion and piety?

Liturgy is the Church's public ritual for worshipping God. Liturgy takes several forms, the most important of which is, of course, the celebration of the Eucharist at Mass. The Church has a rich array of other liturgical prayers as well—the Liturgy of the Hours, Liturgies of the Word, blessings, and other celebrations of the sacraments outside of Mass. The liturgies of the Church are our most important prayers.

But "the spiritual life . . . is not limited solely to participation in the liturgy,"[1] the Fathers of the Second Vatican Council declared. Throughout the world and through the ages, many nonliturgical devotions (sometimes called popular piety) have developed in ways by which the faithful express their love for God. These include prayers like the Rosary, various chaplets, novenas, the Stations of the Cross, as well as prayer in the presence of the Blessed Sacrament.

Of course, the line between liturgy and devotion is often blurry. We bring elements of popular piety with us when we go to Mass. Many of us silently pray "My Lord and my God" as the priest elevates the host and the chalice, a prayer that is not called for in the liturgy, but has become as much a part of the Mass as any other for Catholics. Sometimes popular piety makes its way into the liturgy, as for example when Pope John Paul II declared the Second Sunday of Easter to be the Sunday of Divine Mercy. When it comes to Eucharistic devotions, the line is especially blurry, since the Blessed

---

1 CSL, 12.

Sacrament is inseparable from the celebration of the Eucharist, and periods of adoration begin and end with the celebration of the Mass.

Exposition of the Blessed Sacrament, benediction, and reposition are all liturgy: they are rites of the Church with liturgical norms that must be followed whenever these rites take place and it involves periods of adoration. Adoration of the Blessed Sacrament, on the other hand, can take the form of a liturgy—as when a parish group prays the Liturgy of the Hours before the tabernacle—but it is essentially a devotional practice for which no set form is prescribed by the Church.

Perspective is key. Important as devotions are, liturgy is more important.

"While sacramental actions are *necessary* to life in Christ, the various forms of popular piety are properly *optional*. Such is clearly proven by the Church's precept which obliges attendance at Sunday Mass. No such obligation, however, has obtained with regard to pious exercises, notwithstanding their worthiness or their widespread diffusion."[2]

—————————●●●—————————

In reverent prayer before the reserved Eucharist, the faithful give praise and thanksgiving to Christ for the priceless gift of redemption and for the spiritual food that sustains them in their daily lives. Here they learn to appreciate their right and responsibility to join the offering of their own lives to the perfect sacrifice of Christ during the Mass* and are led to a greater recognition of Christ in themselves and in others, especially in the poor and needy.

—*Built of Living Stones*, 71

Thus all our devotions, including hours of adoration in the presence of the Blessed Sacrament, need to flow from the liturgy, and not vice versa.

"Popular devotions of the Christian people are to be highly endorsed. . . . But these devotions should be so fashioned that they harmonize with the liturgical seasons, accord with the sacred liturgy, are in some way derived from it, and lead the people to it, since, in fact, the liturgy, by its very nature far surpasses any of them."[3]

---

* CSL, 48: "The Church, therefore, earnestly desires that Christ's faithful, when present at this mystery of faith, should not be there as strangers or silent spectators. On the contrary, through a proper appreciation of the rites and prayers they should participate knowingly, devoutly, and actively. They should be instructed by God's word and be refreshed at the table of the Lord's body; they should give thanks to God; by offering the Immaculate Victim, not only through the hands of the priest, but also with him, they should learn to offer themselves too. Through Christ the Mediator, they should be drawn day by day into ever closer union with God and with each other, so that finally God may be all in all."

2 DPPL, 11.
3 CSL, 13.

2. How is prayer in the presence of the Blessed Sacrament related to Mass?

Praying in the presence of the Blessed Sacrament extends the prayers, praise, adoration, and thanksgiving of the Mass and acknowledges the great mystery of Christ's Real Presence in the consecrated bread. As people of faith, we know that this is no "ordinary bread," but Christ — Body, Blood, soul, and divinity. Although the Mass is the "source and summit"[4] of our faith and the most important act of the Christian week, prayer in the presence of the reserved Sacrament "extend[s] the grace of the sacrifice"[5] of the Mass. As Pope Benedict said:

Praying before the Blessed Sacrament leads us to a deeper participation in the Mass, the "source and summit of the Christian life."[7]

"In the Eucharist, the Son of God comes to meet us and desires to become one with us; eucharistic adoration is simply the natural consequence of the eucharistic celebration, which is itself the Church's supreme act of adoration. . . . The act of adoration outside Mass prolongs and intensifies all that takes place during the liturgical celebration itself. . . . And it is precisely this personal encounter with the Lord that then strengthens the social mission contained in the Eucharist, which seeks to break down not only the walls that separate the Lord and ourselves, but also and especially the walls that separate us from one another."[6]

The Mass sends us forth to "glorify the Lord by our life." This includes prayer. We go forth and are led to deeper prayer, and this experience is heightened as we are led back into full participation in the Mass. We are invited further, especially with exposition, "to the spiritual union with [Christ] that culminates in sacramental communion."[8] When we pray in the presence of the Blessed Sacrament:

---

4 LG, 11; see also CSL, 10.
5 HCW, 4
6 SacCar, 66.
7 See CSL, 14.
8 HCW, 82.

"there must be nothing about the appointments used for exposition that could in any way obscure Christ's intention of instituting the eucharist above all to be near us to feed, to heal, and to comfort us."[9]

3. People in my parish just want silence when they come to the chapel to pray before the monstrance. They do not want any distractions with their time with the Lord. What may I do?

Silence is part of the model provided in the ritual books—this is in addition to the inclusion of Scripture readings, music, and prayer texts. *Holy Communion and Worship of the Eucharist* insists:

> "During the exposition there should be prayers, songs, and readings to direct the attention of the faithful to worship of Christ the Lord. . . . It is also desirable for the people to respond to the word of God by singing and to spend some periods of time in religious silence."[10]

The reason for providing a Scripture reading, a song, or a psalm is to stimulate personal and communal prayer. Not everyone is comfortable praying for long periods in the presence of the Blessed Sacrament without some kind of stimulus for

Time for silence should be given so that people may offer personal prayers to God.

their prayer. We should not have too lengthy a period of silence. While this may make people who are comfortable with lengthy periods of silent prayer happy, those who find it difficult to pray for such a long period will not be helped and may give up on praying in the presence of the Blessed Sacrament.

---

9 HCW, 82.
10 HCW, 95.

We need to minister to all the people who have varying needs with personal prayer.

While some people bring prayer books or spiritual reading books, most do not. To be a welcoming community, the Church should make an effort to provide for the needs of all the people in order to facilitate the experience of communion with God during this time of prayer in the presence of the Blessed Sacrament. Those who prepare the liturgy should allow for silence so that people may offer personal prayers to God.

4. Is there much flexibility for creating communal prayer services in the presence of the Blessed Sacrament?

Yes. The liturgical documents published for the United States give an outline and a structure serving as a model for Eucharistic worship outside of Mass. The important point that these documents stress is that communal prayer should include Scripture readings, the singing of hymns, periods of silence, and other prayers.[11]

5. Are priests (pastors) encouraged to promote the practice of praying in the presence of the Blessed Sacrament?

Yes. *Holy Communion and Worship of the Eucharist Outside Mass* states:

"Pastors should see that, unless a serious reason stands in the way, churches where . . . the holy eucharist is reserved, are open every day for at least several hours at a convenient time, so that the faithful may easily pray in the presence of the blessed sacrament."[12]

6. How often should our parish have exposition of the Blessed Sacrament?

It is recommended that a parish provide exposition of the Blessed Sacrament for an appropriate period at least once during the year.[13] It does not need to be an extended service; a brief service is perfectly acceptable.[14] The pastor and the liturgical staff should review the spiritual needs of the parish with

---

11 See page 24.
12 HCW, 8; see also CIC, 937.
13 See HCW, 86, and CIC, 942.
14 See HCW, 86.

the pastoral council and the liturgy commission to determine the appropriate times for exposition.

7. May Mass and exposition occur at the same time?

Holy Communion and Worship of the Eucharist Outside Mass is clear that the primary form of prayer for Catholic Christians is the Mass. The ritual text stresses that Eucharistic piety should never obscure the centrality of the Mass. This is why the celebration of Mass is prohibited at the same time as exposition.[15] *Redemptionis sacramentum* further clarifies: "Holy Mass should be celebrated frequently, even daily if possible, while the Exposition should rigorously be interrupted while Mass is being celebrated."[16]

8. May we have a glass tabernacle or a vessel that may be opened so that people can see the Blessed Sacrament? Or can we insert a glass door within the tabernacle so that the main door of the tabernacle may be left open at all times?

Glass vessels may not be used for the Eucharist—this includes tabernacles, chalices, and ciboria. The leaders of the Church are concerned about the safety of and honor given to the Eucharist. Glass vessels can break or shatter, which desecrates the Sacred Species. Therefore, regulations are put in place to ensure a dignified practice. The Church forbids:

> "The practice of using for the celebration of Mass common vessels, or others lacking in quality, or devoid of all artistic merit or which are mere containers, as also other vessels made from glass, earthenware, clay, or other materials that break easily. This norm is to be applied even as regards metals and other materials that easily rust or deteriorate."[17]

In addition to this:

> "The tabernacle should usually be the only one, be irremovable, be made of solid and inviolable material that is not transparent, and be locked in such a way that the danger of profanation is prevented to the greatest extent possible. Moreover, it is appropriate that before it is put into

---

15 See HCW, 6 and 83; OSE, 8.
16 RS, 140.
17 RS, 117.

liturgical use, the tabernacle be blessed according to the rite described in the Roman Ritual."[18]

A tabernacle should never be made from glass—even inner doors. This secures the Eucharist in a reverent place for reservation and greatly reduces the risk for vandalism and desecration.

9. How many tabernacles are allowed in a parish church?

In churches built before the Second Vatican Council, it was not uncommon to find several "side" altars, in addition to the "main" (or "high") altar at which Mass was usually celebrated. (Especially at schools run by religious communities of priests, several Masses would be celebrated simultaneously at different side altars on weekday mornings.) Often, many of these side altars were equipped with tabernacles, though usually the Blessed Sacrament was reserved in only one tabernacle in a church.[19] Typically, a tabernacle on one side altar was only used when an "altar of repose" was needed on Holy Thursday night to reserve the Sacrament for the Good Friday service.

After the introduction of concelebration as a result of the *Constitution on the Sacred Liturgy* of the Second Vatican Council, and in reflecting on the emphasis found in patristic writings on the one Eucharist around the one altar,[20] multiple altars in a church were considered to be less than ideal, unless they were in self-contained chapels.[21] Also, since altars in new churches were designed so that Mass could be celebrated facing the people, tabernacles were no longer automatically associated with altars. In fact, current liturgical law discourages having a tabernacle containing the Blessed Sacrament on an altar at which Mass is celebrated.[22]

Other legislation promulgated after the Second Vatican Council emphasizes that normally there should be only one tabernacle in a church.[23] Ideally, the space near the tabernacle would be such that the faithful could easily gather there outside of Mass for private prayer.

Examples of separate Blessed Sacrament chapels, which can easily be visited by the faithful even if a liturgy is being celebrated in the body of the church, can be seen in the Cathedral of Our Lady of the Angels in Los Angeles

---

18 GIRM, 314; see also HCW, 10.
19 See CIC, 938 §1.
20 See CSL, 41.
21 See *Rite of Dedication of a Church*, chapter IV, 7; GIRM, 303.
22 See GIRM, 315; EM, 55.
23 See for example, GIRM, 314; EM, 52; HWE, 10.

(where the chapel is near the main doors of the church, but also close to the sanctuary), in St. Patrick's Cathedral in New York (where the Blessed Sacrament is reserved in Our Lady's Chapel behind the main sanctuary), in St. Peter's Basilica in Rome (where the Blessed Sacrament is in a right side chapel about half-way up the nave), as well as in other large churches.

During the Sacred Paschal Triduum, each parish needs to make appropriate arrangements regarding the tabernacle and reserving the Sacrament in line with the liturgies of each day.[24] For example, on Holy Thursday morning, whatever may be reserved in the tabernacle should be removed to a secure location (that is, a locked cupboard in the sacristy or a separate chapel outside the church), so that the tabernacle is, in fact, empty in accordance with the rubrics for the evening Mass of the Lord's Supper.[25] If the usual place for reserving the Blessed Sacrament is not in a distinct chapel, then another appropriate place should be arranged to reserve the Sacrament after the concluding procession and for prayer until midnight.[26] After the liturgy on Good Friday and before the Easter Vigil, the normal place of reservation should not normally be used, and the Sacrament should usually be kept, in case it is needed for Viaticum, in another location outside the body of the church or in the sacristy. Only if there is no other option should the usual tabernacle be used.[27]

Current liturgical norms repeatedly focus on unity and the avoidance of duplications—whether referring to altars, tabernacles, or images in churches.[28] This oneness is meant to help us remember that in our celebration of the Eucharist and in the sharing from the one loaf of bread, we form one body in Christ.[29] Since there is also a diversity of architectural styles (and ages) of the physical churches in which Catholics gather to worship, it is very difficult to give a "one-size-fits-all" answer to questions regarding the location (and number) of tabernacles. The *General Instruction of the Roman Missal* indicates that the location of the tabernacle is up to the judgment of the diocesan bishop, any specific questions should normally be resolved in line with established diocesan policies.[30]

---

24 See also page 55.
25 See *The Roman Missal*: Holy Thursday Mass of the Lord's Supper, 5.
26 See PS, 49.
27 See *The Roman Missal*: Good Friday, 29
28 See GIRM, 318.
29 See 1 Corinthians 10:17.
30 See GIRM, 315.

10. Why is it not considered best practice to retrieve extra hosts from the tabernacle during Mass to distribute during the Communion Rite?

Distributing Holy Communion retrieved from the tabernacle during Mass has always been a concern of the Church. Church documents are clear that consecrated hosts are reserved in the tabernacle for the purpose of Viaticum, to give Communion to the sick and homebound, and for prayer; the reservation is not intended for the distribution of Holy Communion during Mass.[31]

The *Constitution on the Sacred Liturgy* emphasizes that it is a "more complete form of participation in the Mass by which the faithful, after the priest's communion, receive the Lord's body from the sacrifice."[32] The *Constitution* continues to say this practice should be "strongly endorsed."[33] The *General Instruction of the Roman Missal* reiterates the *Constitution*:

> "It is most desirable that the faithful, just as the Priest himself is bound to do, receive the Lord's Body from hosts consecrated at the same Mass and that, in the cases where this is foreseen, they partake of the chalice, so that even by means of the signs Communion may stand out more clearly as a participation in the sacrifice actually being celebrated."[34]

The *General Instruction* presumes that parishes are not distributing Communion during Mass by using the reserved sacraments—it does not provide rubrics or directives for how to do so appropriately.[35]

Redemptionis sacramentum also states:

> "'So that even by means of the signs Communion may stand out more clearly as a participation in the Sacrifice being celebrated,' it is preferable that the faithful be able to receive hosts consecrated in the same Mass."[36]

Although these documents use the phrases (or words) "it is most desirable" and "preferable," thus, suggesting that the practice is not prohibited, the *Norms for the Distribution and Reception of Holy Communion under Both*

---

31 See HCW, 5; EM, 49; BLS, 70; CCC, 1379; *Gathered in Steadfast Faith*, 28, 58.

32 CSL, 55.

33 CSL, 55; see also EM, 31 and 32.

34 GIRM, 85; see also GIRM, 283.

35 This is not a new theology or practice for the Church. The Church has encouraged this practice for centuries. For example, Pope Benedict XIV encouraged the reception of Holy Communion consecrated at the same Mass in his document, *Certiores effecti* (see article 7), promulgated in 1742. This practice was also encouraged by Pope Pius XII in *Mediator Dei* (see article 121), promulgated in 1947.

36 RS, 89.; see also CSL,55, EM, 31 and GIRM, 85, 157, 160, and 243.

Kinds in the Dioceses of the United States of America (a document from the United States Bishops found in *The Roman Missal*) recommends that parishes in the dioceses of the United States do *not* use the reserved Sacrament during Mass as a "general rule."[37]

Of course, there are practical reasons why hosts are needed from the tabernacle during Mass, but these reasons should not validate its frequent practice. Going to the tabernacle during Mass should only occur out of necessity. Parishes should strive to take accurate counts of those attending Mass so that members of the assembly receive hosts that are consecrated at the Mass they are attending. Doing so ensures that their participation in the life-giving meal and sacrifice of the Eucharist is clear, and maintains the connection between the reserved Sacrament as fulfilling the need for Viaticum, receiving Communion when one is ill or homebound, and the need for prayer in the presence of the Blessed Sacrament. The reserved Sacrament should not be a source for Communion during the Mass.

Here are some ideas that will help parishes accurately count those present at Mass in order to ensure that enough hosts are consecrated for distribution of Holy Communion:

- The sacristan should always check to see how full the tabernacle is. Enough hosts should be present for the needs of the dying, sick, and homebound.[38]

- Designate a volunteer (the sacristan or one of the greeters or ushers) to count the number of people present at every Mass (Sunday Mass as well as daily Masses, weddings, funerals, and so on). The sacristan or other volunteer should know how many people the church can seat. This information will be helpful for knowing how many people are in attendance at a particular Mass.

- The numbers for Sunday and weekday Masses should be recorded (perhaps in a spreadsheet) to help provide a base number of hosts and enough wine to be placed in the ciborium before Mass begins.

- A base number of hosts should be placed in ciboria and a base amount of wine in the cruets should be placed on the gifts table before Mass begins.

---

37 *Norms for the Distribution and Reception of Holy Communion under Both Kinds in the Dioceses of the United States of America* (NDRHC), 30.

38 Parishes should know how many hosts they will need during the week for giving Communion to the sick, ill, and homebound. In some cases, priests and deacons may need to consume extra hosts so that the number of hosts stays fairly stable in the tabernacle.

- If more hosts and wine are needed, the sacristan (or other volunteer) adds more hosts to the ciboria and wine to the cruet(s)during the homily or Universal Prayer.

- At daily Masses, funerals, weddings, or other smaller Masses, you can encourage parishioners to place their own host in ciboria that are placed on the gifts table. For health reasons, provide tongs and/or hand sanitation lotion for parishioners to use.

- After a few weeks of keeping track of the numbers of people coming to the various Masses, you will notice a pattern that will make it easier to estimate the number of hosts that you will need to place on the Eucharistic plate or ciboria and the correct ammount of wine in the cruets.[39]

11. Must there always be a sanctuary lamp or candle burning?

There must always be a perpetual flame kept burning near the tabernacle. This points to the presence and holiness of the Blessed Sacrament in the tabernacle.[40]

12. How often should the host be replaced in the luna?

This depends on the climate. In warmer climates, it is best to replace the host at least once a week, especially when they are stored in a metal tabernacle. The hosts can become brittle from the heat. In colder climates, this becomes a seasonal question. During the fall and winter months, you might be able to change the hosts every other week. However, in spring and fall, it is best to change them every week. The basic rule is not to keep the hosts for too lengthy a period in the tabernacle so that it does not become brittle or start to disintegrate. Sometimes, a damp climate can adversely affect the reserved Eucharist. This is another good reason not to consecrate too many hosts and to consume the majority of the hosts consecrated at Mass. When changing the hosts, the host that had been in the luna can be broken and placed in the ciborium in the tabernacle, where it can be distributed to the sick and home-bound. There is no need to immediately consume it. Furthermore, to help

---

39 Of course, other parishes are successful with other practices or options. What is noted above is meant to be a basic guide to use in your parish.

40 See EM, 57 and CIC, 940.

make the connection between the Mass and exposition of the Blessed Sacrament, the host for the luna could be changed each time there is exposition, perhaps even every day, to focus the attention that it is from the Mass that we reserve the Blessed Sacrament.

13. What are adoration "bands" or hours?

Church documents encourage at least two people to be present to pray in the presence of the Blessed Sacrament when it is perpetually exposed. The practice of "bands" or advanced sign-ups for an hour of prayer in the presence of the Blessed Sacrament became necessary in order to determine if parishes had sufficient numbers of people signed up to warrant perpetual exposition, or at least for a lengthy period (several hours). If you do not have sufficient people for a lengthy period of exposition, a parish can still invite people to pray before the tabernacle in churches that are able to be left open for communal and private prayer during the day.[41]

14. May a cover be placed over the monstrance with the exposed Sacrament if someone does not show up for their scheduled prayer time?

The use of a cover or drape may not be used, for this is not the proper form of reposition. The Blessed Sacrament may not be exposed if no one is present. If no one is present, the Blessed Sacrament is removed from the monstrance and placed in the tabernacle—a layperson may do this. Be careful to lock the tabernacle and place the monstrance in a safe place in the sacristy.[42]

15. What are some other styles of prayer in the presence of the Blessed Sacrament, especially when done in common or with a congregation?

- **Taizé**: The term "Taizé" is used to describe the style of prayer that emerged from an ecumenical monastic community in Taizé, France. The brothers of this community have composed short, mantra-like antiphons to be used during the Liturgy of the Hours and other forms of prayer. Familiar "Taizé songs" are "Jesus, Remember Me" and "Eat this Bread." The short refrains are available in multiple languages,

---

41 See page 45.
42 See HCW, 88, 91.

including English, and may be sung repeatedly for communal meditation. The music may be interspersed with extended periods of silence and proclamations from Scripture. The monastic community often gathers in a carefully prepared environment, with a cross centrally located and surrounded by candles, icons, and incense. This type of prayer may be easily adapted with Eucharistic exposition or even adoration before the tabernacle.

- **Lectio divina:** This is a form of biblical spirituality in which a short piece of Scripture is read and then followed by a period of silent reflection. The practice may be repeated several times.

- **The Jesus Prayer**: This prayer is also known as the "Prayer of the Heart" and it is recited as a mantra (much like the Rosary or singing Taizé-style music) with silent pauses interspersed. It may be repeated over a period during a holy hour:

Lord Jesus Christ, Son of God, have mercy on me.

- **Personal Prayer**: One may use their own prayer of preference. It is not communal and does not need a formal structure, style, or text.

- **Liturgy of the Hours**: The prayer of the Church that guides our prayer and praise throughout the day at morning, midday, evening, and before bed. The official ritual of the Church is found in the four-volume set; however, a simple order of prayer is found in many hymnals and music resources. *Christian Prayer* and *Simple Christian Prayer* are simplified editions of the Liturgy of the Hours. The *Order for the Solemn Exposition of the Blessed Sacrament* includes texts for Morning and Evening Prayer that may be done in the presence of the Eucharist.

16. What other opportunities are there for parishes to offer exposition?

As the desire for exposition increases, so do the varied ways that parishes may participate. In March of 2015, Pope Francis asked parishes to be open for a forty hour period with exposition and access to the Sacrament of Reconciliation. Many parishes are beginning to combine exposition and Reconciliation on a weekday evening or on Saturdays. Other parishes prepare these opportunities with particular themes such as a Holy Hour for Life, Religious Freedom, Prayer for Veterans, and the Sunday of Divine Mercy.

Throughout an hour or day of prayer, there may be a Word Service or the Liturgy of the Hours.[43] Many parishes add these times in Advent or Lent, for example on a Wednesday evening or before or after the Stations of the Cross on a Friday. A parish could close the weekend by celebrating Sunday Evening Prayer with exposition. Perhaps during the week, parish grade school children might spend time in the presence of the Blessed Sacrament throughout the morning and end with benediction, or schedule exposition during an evening for religious education students.

High school and college youth programs combine exposition with praise and worship music.[44] Or, if praise and worship music is not a familiar genre for the parish, consider simple Taizé chants; a plaintive Gregorian chant; or unaccompanied cello, recorder, or classical guitar.[45] While these musical elements are rich, do not forget the importance of the element of silence as well.

Of course, when providing exposition for special groups (such as the parish school or youth group), it is best if the invitation is extended to the entire parish community.[46]

17. When I was a child, I remember praying the Divine Praises at benediction. The Divine Praises are not found in the ritual book for the Rite of Exposition and Benediction. Are they still to be done?

The Divine Praises are a series of statements that "bless" different names of the Trinity, Mary, St. Joseph, and other saints. Each statement begins with "Blessed be. . . " The origin of this prayer is not clear. They may have been composed by Louis Felici in 1779 as reparation for blasphemy and profanity. The Divine Praises were eventually added to the prayers at the end of the Mass. Pope Pius VII attached indulgences to them in 1801. They were then attached to benediction, which was done in the United States at the end of high Mass.[47]

Although not found in the post-Conciliar ritual books, the Divine Praises are usually included in annual worship aid resources. Some may feel

---

43 See also page 22.

44 Be sure to evaluate the selections of music according to the musical, pastoral, and liturgical judgments found in *Sing to the Lord: Music in Divine Worship*, 126-135.

45 See also page 40.

46 See also page 21.

47 See *Encyclopedia of Catholicism*, (San Francisco: HarperCollins, 1995).

that this is an appropriate prayer, but it is helpful to remember the context and history of the Divine Praises. Acclamations and responses that focus on the Eucharistic mystery are more appropriate. Scripture, prayer, and music suggestions are provided in *Holy Communion and Worship of the Eucharist Outside Mass* and the *Order for the Solemn Exposition of the Holy Eucharist.*

18. We are a small parish, with a priest who is shared between three other parishes in this rural area. We have always had exposition of the Blessed Sacrament on the first Friday of the month but are looking for a more appropriate way to end the evening. Most months the priest is not available for benediction. What would be a good outline of a ritual for us to use?

An appropriate way to end a day of prayer with exposition of the Blessed Sacrament is to celebrate the ritual found in the *Order for the Solemn Exposition of the Blessed Sacrament* with either Evening Prayer (chapter 2) or the Eucharistic service (see chapter 3). It also might be helpful to read a Eucharistic reflection from one of the many magazines or resources that share insights on the Eucharist, its theology and mission. If your priest (or deacon) is not available, benediction is not included and, instead, a designated lay-person may repose the Blessed Sacrament. Here is a simple closing prayer at the "end of the day" outline[48]:

- Opening Song
- Greeting
- Collect
- Responsorial Psalm
- Reading from Sacred Scripture
- Silence
- A Eucharistic reflection from the Fathers of the Church or current theologian
- Silence

---

48 The outline is based in part on the Eucharistic Services found in chapter 3 of the OSE.

- Prayer of Thanksgiving for the Eucharist
- Intercessions [option to add personal petitions in silence][49]
- The Lord's Prayer
- Reposition of the Blessed Sacrament
- Eucharistic song of praise

19. We celebrate weekday Mass in the main church and then have exposition in the sacrament chapel during the day. Currently, a sacristan takes out the monstrance and places it on the chapel altar while the priest is greeting the people after Mass. Is there another way we do this more reverently?

The ritual books do not provide a specific answer to this question. Using the model provided in the *Order for Solemn Exposition of the Holy Eucharist*,[50] the following could take place: the Blessed Sacrament should be prepared in the luna after the people have received Communion. The deacon or priest places the luna in the monstrance. The Concluding Rites are omitted. Following the Prayer after Communion the celebrant goes to the altar and incenses the Sacrament while a song may be sung. After a short silence, the priest celebrant stands and says a prayer. The procession follows. The procession in the ritual book is usually intended for special occasions, like the procession that occurs on the Solemnity of the Most Holy Body and Blood of Christ (*Corpus Christi*). However, this could be adapted for exposition that is celebrated in a place separate from where the preceding Mass was celebrated, even on weekdays. The ritual states: "The celebrant, wearing either the Mass vestments or a white cope, puts on the humeral veil, and, assisted by the deacon [if there is a deacon], takes the monstrance."[51] Singing may accompany the procession. The monstrance is placed on the altar (a throne may be used) and the period of exposition continues.

---

49 In cases where people are properly catechized about the use of spontaneous petitions (see GIRM, 70), you may invite people to voice their own petitions after the written petitions have been spoken.

50 See OSE, 31-36.

51 OSE, 35.

20. Our parish incorporates a procession after the principal Mass on the Solemnity of the Most Holy Body and Blood of Christ (*Corpus Christi*). Parishioners love this event and the parish council has received a request to host other processions throughout the year. Is this allowed?

The most common day to have a Eucharistic procession is on the Solemnity of the Most Holy Body and Blood of Christ (*Corpus Christi*). With the permission of the bishop, parishes may decide to host additional processions throughout the year. These could be held on the parish's patronal feast day or the anniversary of the parish's dedication. Other parishes in the area could be invited to join the procession. One idea is to have several parishes in the deanery or vicariate coordinate the procession to follow the celebration of Mass on an important feast day. Following the procession, provide an opportunity for exposition and benediction. At the conclusion of Eucharistic exposition and benediction, it would be advisable to have the lay ministers and adult volunteers facilitate small faith-sharing groups, with the participants discussing the Eucharistic worship they just celebrated: Mass and the sharing of Communion, the Eucharistic procession, and Eucharistic exposition. Hence, theological reflection flows from the liturgical experience, presenting a fruitful time for Eucharistic catechesis and liturgical reflection.

With the permission of the bishop, processions may occur on other days.

21. Our parish is not currently offering perpetual exposition. We're not sure if we will be able to secure enough people and would like to begin slowly. What is a good idea?

The high seasons of Advent and Christmas Time, Lent, and Easter Time are wonderful for providing additional options for prayer and for trying to get something off the ground. For example, when Advent begins, combine the celebration of Evening Prayer with exposition and benediction on weekday evenings. Schedule it after the work hour so that more people will be inclined to attend. Exposition could be preceded by a simple parish dinner—soup and bread or a fish fry during Lent, or a potluck during Easter Time. Continue to schedule it weekly during Christmas Time, Ordinary Time, and so on. As interest increases, this will help determine the level of commitment from your parish for perpetual exposition.

22. The teens in our parish have been expressing a desire to have Eucharistic exposition once a month. The youth minister requested that the deacon of the parish preside over the service for the teenagers involved in youth ministry. Graciously, the parish deacon agreed to preside at a monthly exposition service for the teenagers at their regular gathering time. Is it appropriate for teens to have their own service?

In the United States, we have witnessed a growing interest from teens to participate in Eucharistic exposition services both at the parish level and at various youth venues, such as diocesan retreats and rallies, regional meetings and events, and national conferences. As you evaluate how you as a parish will prepare exposition, it is also important to evaluate how you will introduce youth to this practice.

Oftentimes a separate Eucharistic service for young people is scheduled apart from the Sunday assembly. The potential theological danger is that young people are separated from the larger parish community to celebrate a liturgical rite of the Church. This type of monthly ritual is too exclusive to the youth and runs the risk of elitism. It is the responsibility of the youth minister to help connect the larger faith community to the adolescent population of the parish, and the work to ensure that young people are included in the array of liturgical and ministerial opportunities existing in the parish. Youth should always be invited to participate in the liturgical life of the parish; therefore, integration into parish life is essential.

The youth should participate in preexisting parish-wide service of the Rite of Exposition and Benediction and be integrated into the larger faith community. This pastoral solution has three positive liturgical benefits:

- It allows for a youth minister to amalgamate the adolescents of the parish with other lay faithful of the parish community.

- It is intergenerational and helps create a genuine sense of community.

- It exposes young people to an authentic communal liturgical experience that is distinct from the full celebration of the Sunday Eucharist.

Pastors, liturgists, and youth ministers should work together to consider ways to invite youth to be involved with the parish-wide service. The youth minister, with the help of adolescents and in conjunction with the pastor or the parish liturgist, could prepare particular liturgies for all. Therefore, the worship experience would not only be a youth ministry activity, but a worship experience that highlights the gifts and talents of the teenagers. Young people could serve as ministers of hospitality, candle bearers, incense bearers, servers, cantors and musicians, and readers during exposition.

Questions from Parishioners

Parish staffs often receive questions from parishioners about the Blessed Sacrament. The following provide parish staffs with approriate responses to these commonly asked questions.

1. Why do we pray in the presence of the Blessed Sacrament?

Since the early centuries of the Church we have reserved the Eucharist, the Most Blessed Sacrament, because of our confident faith in the words of the Lord: "This is my Body." Christ's presence in the Eucharist is abiding and continuous. His Real Presence in what appears as the form of bread is abiding and continuous. Because of his abiding presence, the Church has reserved the Sacrament for the

We pray before the Blessed Sacrament, because of our belief in the Real Presence of Christ.

dying and the sick. In addition, we reserve the Blessed Sacrament in the tabernacle and expose the Sacrament in a monstrance so that we may have the possibility of presenting ourselves before Christ in prayer.

The gift of the Real Presence of the Lord in our midst enables us to pray and adore our Lord at additional times outside of Mass. These times of prayer do not replace our participation in the Mass, but they enhance it. The most accessible to anyone is a time of personal prayer in a church, chapel, or oratory in the presence of the Blessed Sacrament. Our faith recalls that our Lord is present in the tabernacle.

> Prayer before Christ the Lord sacramentally present extends the union with Christ that the faithful have reached in communion. It renews the covenant that in turn moves them to maintain by the way they live what they have received through faith and the sacrament. . . . All should be eager to do good works and to please God, so that they may seek to imbue the world with the Christian spirit and, in all things, even in the midst of human affairs, to become witnesses of Christ.
>
> —*Holy Communion and Worship of the Eucharist Outside Mass,* 81

2. Why doesn't the Church reserve the Precious Blood?

The Church has never reserved the Precious Blood, except for the needs of the sick. This is to show respect for the Sacrament because wine can easily spoil and be spilled. If consecrated wine remains after Mass, it is to be consumed immediately and should not be poured into the ground or into the sacrarium.[52]

> "The Precious Blood may not be reserved, except for giving Communion to someone who is sick. Only sick people who are unable to receive Communion under the form of bread may receive it under the form of wine alone at the discretion of the Priest. If not consecrated at a Mass in the presence of the sick person, the Blood of the Lord is kept in a properly covered vessel and is placed in the tabernacle after Communion. The Precious Blood should be carried to the sick in a vessel that is closed in such a way as to eliminate all danger of spilling. If some of the Precious Blood remains after the sick person has received Communion, it should be consumed by the minister, who should also see to it that the vessel is properly purified."[53]

52 See the USCCB website regarding "Reserving the Precious Blood," http://www.usccb.org/prayer-and-worship/the-mass/order-of-mass/liturgy-of-the-eucharist/reserving-the-precious-blood.cfm. Accessed February 18, 2015.

53 NDRHC, 54.

3. What happens when we pray in the presence of the Blessed Sacrament?

Praying in the presence of the Blessed Sacrament extends the benefits of grace received at Mass. When we pray in the presence of the Sacrament, we continue to contemplate Christ's Paschal Mystery. We also recognize our own participation in the Paschal Mystery; that is, how we die to ourselves so that we may be imitators of Christ. The presence of Christ transforms us and changes us so that we are conformed more into his image. This is a powerful mystery and we need further time in our lives to pray with these ideals, beyond Mass.

4. My church offers perpetual exposition. What am I supposed to do to prepare for and pray in the presence of the Blessed Sacrament?

Please note that parish practices may vary but here is a good suggestion: When a parish provides perpetual exposition it is important to show up for your scheduled time. Preparation begins at home, dressing and readying one's self to come to church and to the Blessed Sacrament chapel. Dress appropriately for church: if you tend to be cold, bring a sweater; if you tend to be warm, bring a hand fan. Pray for a safe trip to the church. Arrive five minutes before your scheduled time. If necessary, for security reasons, remember the code to enter the church or chapel.

When you are at church, many parishes have a prayer partner or someone who comes before or after a certain time slot. Decide on an appropriate place and time to meet each week to wait for each other. This might be in the parking lot or vestibule or narthex of the church. Check the lighting and adjust it accordingly. (Some parishes allow you to adjust it, others have it preset.) When at church, check the bulletin board in the vestibule for announcements or notices that may affect your time praying in the presence of the Blessed Sacrament. Look at the church pamphlet rack for Eucharistic reading material if needed. With your prayer partner, walk together to the Blessed Sacrament chapel, making sure that you genuflect or bow before the Blessed Sacrament and to the altar if you pass before it. Sign your name in the record book located on the small table in the chapel. Greet those who have been praying and decide together on a prayer, song, or Scripture passage that you would like to say together at the hour/shift change. A good suggestion is the Lord's Prayer or the Glory Be. Share the Sign of Peace or some other "farewell." When you are at church, use a particular prayer style or format that helps you deepen your love of God.

5. May I say a novena while I pray in the presence of the Blessed Sacrament?

Novenas are often for a specific purpose. A novena is a devotional prayer or worship practice over a period (usually nine days, hours, weeks, and/or months) for a particular prayer intention or need, and may be recited while praying in the presence of the Blessed Sacrament.

6. How and when do I genuflect?

Bending one knee to touch the ground shows reverence to the Blessed Sacrament. Before the Second Vatican Council, it was a common practice for many to use both knees and kneel. This rubric changed with the 1973 ritual book, *Holy Communion and Worship of the Eucharist Outside Mass*. It is usually the practice to genuflect before the Blessed Sacrament. If the Blessed Sacrament is reserved behind the altar in the main worship space we genuflect. Otherwise, if the tabernacle is not behind the altar or off to the side of the altar we bow to the altar and genuflect to the tabernacle. If someone is not able to genuflect, they may make a profound bow or nod their head in reverence.

7. Are prayers in honor of the Blessed Virgin Mary (such as the Rosary) or the saints allowed during exposition of the Blessed Sacrament?

Yes and no. In the late 1960s, the Congregation for the Discipline of the Sacraments answered "no" to the queries.[54] However, St. Pope John Paul II allowed the Rosary to be recited during exposition of the Blessed Sacrament, especially in light of the new mysteries he initiated, addressed to highlight Christ's manifestations.[55] Furthermore, the United States Bishops' Committee

---

54 See *Notitiae* 4 (1968): 133–134.

55 See *Notitiae* (1998): 507–511.

on Divine Worship addressed the question a little further, directing that one may not expose the Eucharist *only* to recite the Rosary.[56] As far as prayers to saints goes, Exposition highlights Christ's Real Presence and our prayers should have this focus as our overall goal and purpose.

---

56 See BCL *Newsletter*, January-February 1999.

RESOURCES

Church Documents and Ritual Books

- *Built of Living Stones.* United States Conference of Catholic Bishops, 2000. This document provides practical guidance and theological explanations for renovating or building churches. Certain paragraphs assist in the placement of the tabernacle and the Eucharistic chapel. This document is found in *The Liturgy Documents, Volume I: Fifth Edition* published by Liturgy Training Publications.

- *Catechism of the Catholic Church: Second Edition.* Washington, DC: United States Conference of Catholic Bishops, 1997. This is the official *Catechism* promulgated in English by Pope John Paul II in 1994 and then updated in 1997. The *Catechism* is an excellent resource for Eucharistic theology, history, and reflection. The paragraphs devoted to Eucharist (§1322—1419) include footnotes from the treasury of our Roman Catholic tradition and wisdom of many writers. Additionally, the *Catechism* makes clear the relationship between the Eucharist as "the source and summit"[1] of our lives and living the Eucharist in the world.

- *Catholic Household Blessings & Prayers.* Washington, DC: United States Conference of Catholic Bishops, 2007. This is a prayer and ritual book for every Catholic family and home. It guides families through the rich heritage of our liturgical year and treasury of prayers.

- *Code of Canon Law: Latin-English Edition.* Washington, DC: Canon Law Society of America, 1983. A comprehensive volume including the major Church laws and legal principles directing the mission of the Catholic Church (Latin or Roman Rite). The *Code* guides how the Church functions, and governs the celebration of the sacraments,

---

1 LG, 11; see also CSL, 14.

the role of "the People of God," and the structures that are important to the Church's life.

- *Directory on Popular Piety and the Liturgy: Principles and Guidelines,* 2002. This document provides guidelines for the devotional life of the Church, emphasizing that all devotions are to be in harmony with the liturgy and the liturgical year. A very complete list of devotions is included. This document is found in *The Liturgy Documents, Volume IV* published by Liturgy Training Publications.

- *Eucharisticum mysterium,* 1967. Pope Paul VI promulgated this document to assist with the liturgical reform and to emphasize the importance of the Eucharist and the Order of Mass. It is a notable Eucharistic reflection. It is found in *The Liturgy Documents, Volume III* published by Liturgy Training Publications.

- *General Instruction of the Roman Missal,* 2010. This is the "road map" document that helps facilitate the celebration of the Mass. Each part of the Mass is explained in ritual detail, with theological explanations for the various parts of the Mass. It is found in *The Roman Missal* and *The Liturgy Documents, Volume I* published by Liturgy Training Publications.

- *Holy Communion and Worship of the Eucharist Outside Mass,* 1994. The official document from the Congregation for Divine Worship and Discipline of the Sacraments regarding exposition of the Blessed Sacrament and the other practices related to worship of the Eucharist outside of Mass. It is available in *The Liturgy Documents, Volume II* published by Liturgy Training Publications.

- *Mysterium fidei,* 1965. This document focuses on the importance of the Eucharist and its celebration, the importance of communal celebrations of the Mass, and the valid teachings on the Eucharist.

- *The Order for Solemn Exposition of the Holy Eucharist.* Collegeville, Minnesota: The Liturgical Press, 1993. The official ritual book for exposition that the BCL (now BCDW) published for the Dioceses of the United States of America. The Vatican document, *Holy Communion and Worship of the Eucharist Outside Mass* requested that bishops' conferences publish ritual books for their own countries. The BCL developed and approved this ritual book that was published by Liturgical Press in 1993.

- *Redemptionis sacramentum*, 2004. This document was issued by the Congregation for Divine Worship and the Discipline of the Sacraments. It assists the bishops of the world with updated rubrics for the celebration of the Mass and other types of Eucharistic worship.

- *The Roman Missal*, third edition, 2011. The ritual book including rubrics, prayer texts, and governing documents for the celebration of the Mass. It is available from seven Catholic publishers, including Liturgy Training Publications.

- *Sacramentum caritatis*, 2007. This postsynodal apostolic exhortation from Pope Benedict XVI includes wonderful reflections on the Eucharist and the relationship of the Mass to living our faith in the world.

- *Sacrosanctum Concilium, 1963*. As the first document issued from the Second Vatican Council, the *Constitution* serves as the "magna carta" for liturgical reform. It is often referred to by its English title, the *Constitution on the Sacred Liturgy*.

Theological and Historical Resources

- *Days of the Lord, The Liturgical Year: Volume 7, Solemnities and Feasts*. Collegeville, Minnesota: The Liturgical Press, 1994. This excellent series comes from France and was translated into English. This particular volume includes background information about the Solemnity of the Most Holy Body and Blood of Christ (*Corpus Christi*).

- Dudley, Martin R. "Liturgy and Doctrine: Corpus Christi," *Worship* 66 (1992), pages 417–426. Presents a history of the Solemnity of the Most Holy Body and Blood of Christ (*Corpus Christi*) and the practices that surround this liturgical observance.

- Falardeau, sss, Ernest. *One Bread and Cup: Source of Communion*. Collegeville, Minnesota: The Liturgical Press, 1987. A theological and ecumenical study of the Eucharist.

- Foley, Edward. *From Age to Age: How Christians Have Celebrated the Eucharist* (Revised and Expanded Edition). Collegeville, Minnesota: The Liturgical Press, 2009. This second edition provides an excellent overview of the history of the Mass, from its Jewish roots to present day.

- Jasper, R.C.D. and Cuming, G.J. *Prayers of the Eucharist, Early and Reformed* (third edition). Collegeville, Minnesota: The Liturgical Press (Pueblo Books), 1987. An historical and theological overview of the Eucharistic Prayers.

- Lane, sss, John Thomas. "From *Corpus Christi* to the Solemnity of the Most Holy Body and Blood of Christ," *Emmanuel Magazine,* June 1997. Provides a detailed historical and theological overview of this solemnity, including a practical reflection on its post-Conciliar celebration.

- ____ . "Why don't we distribute Holy Communion from the tabernacle during Mass?" *Emmanuel Magazine,* July 2007. This article reminds us of the importance of receiving Holy Communion from the same Mass and not from a previous celebration.

- LaVerdiere, sss, Eugene. *The Eucharist in the New Testament and the Early Church*. Collegeville, Minnesota: The Liturgical Press, 1996. Father LaVerdiere was a master storyteller and author. His in-depth Scripture study of the Eucharist is important to review for a clearer vision of the Eucharist in the New Testament and the early Church.

- Macy, Gary. *The Banquet's Wisdom: A Short History of the Theologies of the Lord's Supper*. New York, NY: Paulist Press, 1992. An historical resource focusing on the theological studies of the early Church's Eucharistic practices.

- Martimort, A.G., ed. *The Church at Prayer, Volume 4: The Liturgy and Time*. Collegeville, Minnesota: The Liturgical Press, 1986. This series is another excellent resource for the history of the liturgy. The fourth volume focuses on the Solemnity of the Most Holy Body and Blood of Christ (Corpus Christi).

- Mitchell, Nathan. *Cult and Controversy: The Worship of the Eucharist Outside Mass*. Collegeville, Minnesota: The Liturgical Press (Pueblo Books), 1982. This is the hallmark and penultimate history of worship of the Eucharist outside of Mass.

- Rubin, Miri. *Corpus Christi: The Eucharist in Late Medieval Culture*. Cambridge, England: Cambridge University Press, 1992. This scholarly work presents a detailed history of the Solemnity of the Most Holy Body and Blood of Christ (*Corpus Christi*), from the early visions for this "idea feast," expansion across Europe, promulgation for the entire

Church, and the culture, devotion, and theology that drove the practices surrounding this feast.

- Seasoltz, OSB, R. Kevin, ed. *Living Bread, Saving Cup.* Collegeville, Minnesota: The Liturgical Press, 1982. A compilation of articles regarding the Eucharist as previously published in the liturgical journal *Worship.*

Pastoral Resources

- Bishops' Committee on the Liturgy (BCL). *Newsletter, December 2006.* Washington, DC: United States Conference of Catholic Bishops. Each month the Bishops' Committee on Divine Worship (BCDW) releases a *Newsletter.* When the United States Conference of Catholic Bishops reorganized in 2007, they changed the title of the office for "liturgy" to the office for "divine worship," to be in tandem with the Vatican offices. This particular issue focused on exposition of the Blessed Sacrament and was a reference for this book.

- O'Toole, James M., ed. *Habits of Devotion: Catholic Religious Practice in Twentieth-Century America.* Ithaca, New York: Cornell University Press, 2004. A historical study of the development of Catholic piety.

- Phan, Peter C., ed. *Directory on Popular Piety and the Liturgy: Principles and Guidelines–A Commentary.* Collegeville, Minnesota: The Liturgical Press, 2005. An excellent resource to review with the 2002 Vatican document.

- *Popular Devotional Practices: Basic Questions & Answers.* Washington, DC: United States Conference of Catholic Bishops, 2003. This pamphlet gives succinct answers regarding worship of the Eucharist outside of Mass and other devotions that are not liturgical rites.

- *Thirty-One Questions on Adoration of the Blessed Sacrament: A Resource of the Bishops' Committee on the Liturgy.* Washington, DC: United States Conference of Catholic Bishops, 2004. Questions and answers about Eucharistic adoration.

- *The Real Presence of Jesus Christ in the Sacrament of the Eucharist: Basic Questions & Answers.* Washington, DC: United States Conference of Catholic Bishops, 2001. A helpful tool to review the basic tenets of the Catholic faith in Christ's presence in the Eucharist.

GLOSSARY

Adoration: A form of prayer in the presence of the Blessed Sacrament that is either exposed in a monstrance or reposed in the tabernacle. Adoration involves glorifying God as an extension of the prayers of the Mass. Additionally, it is a style of prayer, made popular in the Western Church (Roman Rite), where one keeps vigil in prayer until the Lord's return.

Alb: A white, liturgical garment that may be worn by all the baptized.

Baldacchino: A type of ornamental fabric, metal, or stone frame that may or may not be held permanently over the altar or throne to highlight the importance of the Blessed Sacrament. It is used in processions with the Eucharist.

Benediction: Blessing with the Blessed Sacrament that ends exposition. It is only offered by an ordained minister (priest or deacon).

Blessed Sacrament: In the Roman Catholic tradition, this is another term used to refer to the consecrated Eucharist.

Canopy: An ornamental covering made from cloth that is hung or held over the monstrance containing the Blessed Sacrament.

Cassock: A full-length garment worn by clerics to signify a particular office or role within the church. It can be black, violet, red, or white.

Chaplet: A string of beads used for counting prayers.

Chasuble: A sleeveless outer vestment worn by a Catholic priest when celebrating the Mass.

Ciborium: A liturgical vessel that holds multiple hosts. From the Latin word *cibus*, meaning "food."

Cope: A long, loose cloak worn by priests or bishops for special ceremonies or rituals such as exposition of the Blessed Sacrament or the Liturgy of the Hours.

Dalmatic: A wide-sleeved vestment worn by a deacon for Mass or other liturgical rites.

Eucharistic Blessing: See "Benediction." The *Order for Solemn Exposition of the Holy Eucharist* uses the term Eucharistic blessing instead of benediction.

Eucharistic Congress: A local or international gathering of study on and prayer with the Eucharist.

Eucharistic Procession: The clergy and the faithful walking in an orderly way—through the church or through the community—with the Blessed Sacrament.

Eucharistic Sacrifice: A theological aspect of the Eucharist—both in Mass and in worship outside Mass—that focuses on Christ's dying on the Cross for our salvation, forgiveness of sins, and renewal of our lives. From the Latin word *sacrificare* meaning "to make holy or sanctify."

Evening Prayer: Official prayer of the Church, also known as Vespers or Evensong. This prayer highlights the thanksgiving of the day, its work, and prays for those who have died and gone before us in faith. Exposition of the Eucharist can be combined with Evening Prayer.

Exposition: The liturgical rite in which the consecrated host is placed in the monstrance for prayer.

Forty Hours: This period of devotional prayer remembers the hours that Jesus laid in the tomb. In former times, there were readings, sermons, hymns, and other ceremonies performed with extended periods of silence and personal prayer. Today, this devotion often occurs during a parish mission or retreat, and is usually not forty consecutive hours.

Genuflection: The bending of the knee to the ground or floor to show reverence and respect to the Blessed Sacrament.

Humeral Veil: A plain piece of narrow cloth that covers the shoulders and hands while holding a monstrance during exposition, benediction, or a Eucharistic procession.

Litany: A series of petitions with a repeated response.

Liturgy of the Hours: The official public prayer of the Church that marks the hours of the day at morning, midmorning, midday, midafternoon, evening, and night. All clerics are obligated to pray the Hours and the faithful are encouraged to pray the hymns, psalms, canticles, readings, and intercessions. Many churches or communities, especially with religious orders of sisters, nuns, brothers, monks, and presbyters, encourage common celebration for all to join. Also referred to as the Divine Office.

Luna: A glass vessel with a special door, usually round, that holds the host, and is placed in a monstrance for exposition of the Blessed Sacrament.

Monstrance: A liturgical vessel designed to hold a single (larger) host, recently consecrated at Mass to foster prayer in the presence of the Blessed Sacrament. From the Latin word *monstrare,* which means "to show." This decorative vessel is placed on the altar to help people who pray make the connection between the Mass and our extended prayer life.

Morning Prayer: The official prayer of the Church at the beginning of the day. We give praise to Christ who illuminates our day and gives us new life.

Novena: A devotional prayer that is prayed over a period (usually nine days, hours, weeks, and/or months, etc.) for a particular prayer intention or need.

Oratory: A small place or chapel for worship, usually found in a religious order's home, that may or may not have a tabernacle for reservation of the Blessed Sacrament.

Paschal Mystery: A theological term referring to Christ's Passion, Death, and Resurrection. We share in Christ's Paschal Mystery through our Baptism.

Perpetual Adoration: An extended period of prayer before the Blessed Sacrament reserved in the tabernacle.

Perpetual Exposition: The Eucharist is exposed in the monstrance for an extended period. The practice requires permission from the local bishop.

Reposition: A liturgical rite for when the Blessed Sacrament is returned to the tabernacle.

Rite or Ritual: A way of praying with a set form or order of service.

Solemn Exposition: The formal Rite of Exposition.

Spiritual Communion: Unifying oneself to Christ in prayer if unable to to physically receive the Blessed Sacrament in Holy Communion.

Stole: A strip of fabric, like a scarf, that is worn over the shoulders to signify ordination. This fabric also marks the liturgical season by its color.

Surplice: A loose white garment that is worn over a cassock. It is usually hip-length.

Tabernacle: A fixed vessel or cabinet, usually on a stand or niche of a wall, that is made to hold the reserved Blessed Sacrament, multiple ciboria with consecrated hosts for the sick, and for prayer.

Vesture (Garment): Liturgical clothing such as an alb, surplice, dalmatic, chasuble, and humeral veil. The garment worn signifies the ministry or office held in the Church.

ACKNOWLEDGMENTS

I am grateful to Danielle A. Noe and Liturgy Training Publications (LTP) for the opportunity to write on this topic. At the beginning, Danielle and my classmate D. Todd Williamson saw a road map and vision for this project.

Through the Southwest Liturgical Conference (SWLC), and especially thanks to the efforts of Sr. Lois Paha, op, its past president, and Rev. James Burkart, its current president, I was able to share these notes for many workshops on this topic. I was honored to serve on the SWLC board for seventeen years, and I shared the special charism of St. Peter Julian Eymard and the Congregation of the Blessed Sacrament. My notes further developed through the many wonderful participants who shared their love of the Eucharist with me.

I am thankful for my religious superiors, especially the Very Rev. Norman Pelletier, sss; Rev. Anthony Schueller, sss; Rev. William Fickel, sss; Rev. Michael Arkins, sss; and Rev. Dana G. Pelotte, sss, for their encouragement, support, and approved sabbatical to complete *Guide for Celebrating® Worship of the Eucharist Outside Mass.*

Along with our Creator, my parents, Jo Ann and John Lane, dreamed me into being, ensured a liturgical life for me, involved our family in parish life, and hosted liturgical committee meetings in our home so that I would know the "source and summit" (*Lumen gentium*, 11) of the Church, and grow to share it with others. I am blessed by their teachings, which have inspired me to learn and grow with fellow sojourners on this great journey of faith.

Dynamic friends and editors have helped me with my "challenged writing ability" to share this faith. Through the grace of Beverly Svoboda, Kathleen Seaman, Olive Balla, Diana Turney, Tomás Luna, Gene LaVerdiere, sss; Anthony Schueller, sss; Paul Bernier, sss; Mona Grigsby Suarez, and Karen Girard, I have been shaped to be a servant of the Word, so that I may work each day writing for the glory of God. I am a richly blessed religious and presbyter today because of my wonderful religious life family and parishioners who have served with me in the (Arch)Dioceses of Cleveland, Green Bay, Chicago, Galveston-Houston, Salt Lake City, and Santa Fe. For their presence in my life, I am most grateful and bring them to this communion at the Table of the Lord.

Let us contemplate this way of prayer together and grow in the mystery of God's love. Let us continue to find Christ who will lead us to the Father and Holy Spirit—a communion of love.

John Thomas Lane, sss
December 9, 2012
Optional Memorial of St. Juan Diego
The 50th Anniversary of the Canonization of St. Peter Julian Eymard,
Apostle of the Eucharist,
and conclusion of the First Session of the
Second Vatican Council